She's
Twelve
going on
Twenty

She's *Twelve* going on *Twenty*

Nurturing Your Daughter
Through the Tween Years

Kim Camp

THOMAS NELSON
Since 1798

NASHVILLE DALLAS MEXICO CITY RIO DE JANEIRO

Published in Nashville, Tennessee, by Thomas Nelson. Thomas Nelson is a registered trademark of Thomas Nelson, Inc.

Thomas Nelson, Inc., titles may be purchased in bulk for educational, business, fund-raising, or sales promotional use. For information, please e-mail SpecialMarkets@ThomasNelson.com.

Unless otherwise noted, Scripture quotations are from the New American Standard Bible®, Copyright © 1960, 1962, 1963, 1968, 1971, 1972, 1973, 1975, 1977, 1995 by The Lockman Foundation. Used by permission. (www.Lockman.org)

Scripture quotations marked NIV are taken from the Holy Bible, New International Version®, NIV®. Copyright © 1973, 1978, 1984, 2011 by Biblica, Inc.™ Used by permission of Zondervan. All rights reserved worldwide. www.zondervan.com

Scripture quotations marked NKJV are taken from the New King James Version®. © 1982 by Thomas Nelson, Inc. Used by permission. All rights reserved.

Scripture quotations marked PHILLIPS are taken from J. B. Phillips: THE NEW TESTAMENT IN MODERN ENGLISH, Revised Edition. © J. B. Phillips 1958, 1960, 1972. Used by permission of Macmillan Publishing Co., Inc.

ISBN 978-0-8499-6487-9 (TP)

Library of Congress Cataloging-in-Publication Data

Camp, Kim, 1963-
She's twelve going on twenty / Kim Camp.
p. cm.
Includes bibliographic references.
ISBN 0-8499-3759-0
Teenage girls—Religious life. 2. Teenage girls—Conduct of life. 3. Mothers and daughters.
4. Parenting—Religious aspects—Christianity. I. Title.
BV4551.2.C32 2000
248.8'431—dc21   99-059373
                                                           CIP

Printed in the United States of America
13 14 15 16 17 QVS 5 4 3 2 1

Contents

Part III: Body

Contents

Introduction

Defining the Dream

*Now may the God of peace Himself sanctify you
entirely; and may your spirit and soul and body be
preserved complete, without blame at the coming of
our Lord Jesus Christ. Faithful is He who calls you,
and He also will bring it to pass.*

—1 Thessalonians 5:23–24

Spirit. Soul. Body. The words are familiar to adults—we
hear them all the time. But what do these three aspects
of human life mean to young girls? How can our daughters
relate to God and to other people spiritually? How can they
understand the importance of feeding and tending their souls?

How can they honor their bodies and see them as God's house on earth, the temple of the Holy Spirit?

Moms and their girls sometimes have a hard time being, and staying, close to each other. One mom told me that some alien something took over her daughter from ages thirteen to seventeen—and then suddenly she got her daughter back. How much I could relate! When I was a teenager, there were times my mom would say I was that kind of daughter. Years later, I became comfortable being the confidante of other women's daughters, someone girls could trust with any kind of information. My goal was always to help daughters communicate with their mothers in a loving and nondefensive way. I also encouraged moms to give their daughters the freedom to share openly without feeling threatened.

I do think that it is important for girls to have other positive role models in their lives, and I felt very grateful to be one for so many girls. But once I had children—including two daughters—of my own, my role shifted. I changed from being a confidante to being a mother.

For fifteen years, I had the incredible privilege of counseling and discipling junior high and high school girls through church and other organizations. But after my fourth child was born, I realized the ultimate act of discipleship for a mom is leading her own children. I felt like I knew firsthand about being the liaison between a young girl and her mom, but to be the mom myself seemed a bit scary. I anticipated a rocky road and began to wonder how it would be to switch roles. Would God provide someone for my girls like I had been for other people's daughters? I didn't want the same scenarios to happen with my girls that had transpired with so many other moms and daughters.

My oldest daughter was just about the age of the girls I'm talking about in this book—nine years old—when I originally wrote the manuscript. The thought on my mind then was, *how can I keep her as close to me as she is today?*

Around that time, she showed me where to find the key to her diary, and asked me to make sure no one reads it except her dad and me.

"Why is it okay for your parents to read it?" I asked. "You can keep it just for your private thoughts."

"Because you are my parents," she said, "and you know everything about me anyway."

There's still a lot of trust between moms and daughters at age nine. But the more I talked to girls, the more I realized that things can damage trust during the perilous passage of adolescence. As mothers, it's vital to focus faithfully and diligently to keep our daughters' confidence and remain trustworthy in their eyes.

In all my conversations with adolescent girls, I've learned how important it is for our daughters to have privacy—to enjoy thoughts and conversations that are theirs alone. Yet within that freedom, they also need to feel free to talk to us, knowing that they can express anything, no matter how scary it may seem, and still receive our love, not our condemnation.

As my relationship with people's daughters created a platform, it led to opportunities to speak at their PTA meetings, youth groups, and parent conferences. After becoming an author, the doors opened to speak regularly throughout the country to school and church groups made up exclusively of junior high and high school girls. These opportunities provided the chance to survey hundreds of teenage girls, read their responses, written in their own words, and write about what they consider to be the most important issues.

They've talked to me about their lives, their problems, their fears, and their dreams. And they've talked to me about their mothers.

Thirteen-year-old Amanda asked me a question that I bet I've heard a hundred times: *"Why is it that everyone can understand me better than my own mom?"*

For years I had wondered why adolescent girls and their mothers have so many problems. Have you wondered about that too? Believe me: once I had daughters of my own, I was more committed than ever to finding the answer.

Of course, sometimes girls forget that their moms are people too. People with schedules and commitments. People with hopes and dreams. People with strengths and weaknesses. People to whom God has given the enormous responsibility for the well-being of their sons and daughters. Fortunately, He has always made His wisdom available to mothers, as well as a little extra bonus of mothers' intuition.

A number of books, including a bestseller called *Reviving Ophelia*,[1] express a movement called "Girl Power," which highlights developing the unique nature and potential of girls. Because I love young girls, and because I've worked with girls ages nine to sixteen for so many years, I applaud this movement. However, while I agree that raising daughters in a climate of "unlimited potential" is exhilarating, I want to join you, mother to mother, in helping our daughters build a firm foundation in Christ. It is my heart's desire, my dream and God's dream, to see our daughters grow up knowing that they can do all things *through Christ*. Rather than pursuing Girl

Power, I hope that we—mothers and daughters alike—will work together to develop *God Power* in our lives, because our greatest potential will always be found in Christ.

So, in the pages that follow, we will explore the best possible ways to communicate with our daughters on such topics as peer influence, music and the media, competition and conflict with friends, drugs and alcohol, sex and purity, and diet and exercise (including eating disorders). This book was born with the hope that as I've been seeking answers as a mom, I would be able to share the invaluable lessons I've learned, not only from some very articulate young girls, but also from insightful and gifted role models who have helped to shape my own view of parenting. One of those role models is Ruth Bell Graham.

My grandfather was on Billy Graham's board for more than forty years, so the Grahams have been a part of my life since childhood. For years I didn't even realize what a privilege it was to spend time with their family. One summer Billy Graham was holding a crusade in Amsterdam and our entire family went over for the week. I was a young woman with questions about life and motherhood, so it was a beautiful gift to spend time with Ruth Graham. Growing up, I knew her as one of my grandmother's friends, but with becoming a mom on the horizon, I saw her as a wise woman who had raised five children of her own and who could surely offer valuable advice!

It was 10:00 p.m. in Amsterdam, yet the sky was still light as if it were an early Texas evening. After the crusade, we sat down for dinner on the hotel veranda, which overlooked a beautiful lake. Children were still playing in the water. Ruth and I talked for a while on several subjects. Finally I asked her something that had been heavy on my heart. "How did you keep a close relationship with the Lord while you were raising all of your children? To me it seems impossible to have the kind of time I need with the Lord to grow in life and also take care of my children."

She shared something with me that I will never forget. "When you are a mother," she explained, "your time is not your own. Your time with the Lord will change for a season, but God knows your heart and He will provide for time with Him." She went on to say that she always kept an open Bible on her desk in the family room and read to herself and to her children at every opportunity.

This counsel has been a great help to me over the years as I've become overwhelmed with the task of balancing life and motherhood. Because of Ruth Graham's words, I've kept a Bible on my kitchen table, and every day God provides some chance for me to sit down and read, gleaning wisdom and strength from His Word. What could be more important?

God has also taught me so much about prayer and especially about specifically praying for my children! Without being in God's Word and in consistent daily prayer, life would be impossible. The last decade has been a wild roller-coaster ride I would not wish on anyone, even though I wouldn't trade even one second. Following the first release of this book, when my kids were ages six to twelve, I went through a very unfortunate divorce from their father. Joining the ranks of single motherhood created a whole new set of challenges, and navigating an unfamiliar course has been an interesting adventure. This edition of the book includes my experiences so far as a single mom, with children now ages seventeen to twenty-three. Sprinkled through these chapters are discussions dealing with two households, coping with scenarios specific to a divorced or blended family, and negotiating dating as a single mom at the same time my children are entering the dating world. I hope the stories will reinforce that if you're raising a daughter in a single-parent household, you are not alone.

How healing it is now to revisit the pages of this book and express new thoughts and ideas. Besides adding stories from a single mom's perspective, I have included a few insights from a male perspective. Our girls need guys who will pursue them in a healthy way, guys who have been taught how to lead and love within God's calling and purpose. They're sometimes hard to find—but the guys say it's hard to find girls who are seeking God and also have standards.

I've learned a lot from living through and being in the midst of life with five teenagers. While focusing on this manuscript, I realized that the truths believed to be woven into the fabric of my being were sometimes totally forgotten in the chaotic moments of the last decade. Living out the truth and knowing it are two different things that work best in tandem. The only way to connect them, I finally sort of understand—at least at this instant—is to cling to the Lord, who then connects them and lives the truth out through us and often in spite of us. We are such well-meaning souls with a great inability to act on our good intentions. Thus our desperate need for our living God to intervene and, in His grace and mercy, weave the beautiful tapestry of our lives that He so clearly sees.

As moms in various walks of life, we all can stand on the foundational principles God gives us in His Word. It is through the truth of God's Word, through the words of other mothers, and through the words of young girls themselves that

I have written the following chapters. We live in a complex and sometimes frightening world. But through Scripture, godly principles, and sensible habits, by God's grace we can build relationships with our girls that will withstand whatever challenges the world may send our way. I believe that in our efforts as mothers, He is able to do a mighty work in us—spirit, soul, and body. He has an incredible plan for each of our lives. And He will, indeed, bring it to pass.

Spirit

Spirit, soul, and body are intertwined so that, when functioning in a healthy way, they balance and support one another. And when we fall into habitual unhealthy habits, our entire person is affected. To better understand how each area operates most effectively, this book is divided into three parts: "Spirit," "Soul," and "Body."

God's Spirit is the vital, animating force of our lives. It is the key to unlocking the door to a healthy body and soul. The various aspects of the body and soul make up the unique keyhole of a door. All the grooves are in place, but they have no purpose without the key. When the Spirit fits perfectly into the keyhole and is joined to our human spirit, all three areas function together to open this door. In this section we will reflect upon this key to our lives, a healthy spirit. As we look deeper we will discover that turning the "key" and unlocking this door is not the passage to perfection, but it is certainly the path to peace.

Who Am I?

H ave you seen the Disney movie *Anastasia*? It is the story of a ten-year-old Russian princess who is separated from her family. Anastasia receives a wound to her head and is left with amnesia. By the time she reaches the age of eighteen, she longs to know who she is and hopes to find a better life. On her search she discovers her true identity and finds her true love. Finding the truth about her heritage replaces yearning and confusion with belonging and the seeds of confidence. The girl who emerges, although timid in confidence, is very strong in character. She has found her identity.[1]

Anastasia certainly isn't the only one on an identity quest. Recently I read about a club for loners. To join, an applicant must write to a certain address and explain why she (or he) enjoys being alone. In return she will receive "loner paraphernalia," the assurance that her name will be included on an exclusive list, and the promise that—once identified as a loner—she will be left alone. Even the most reclusive and withdrawn people in our society need to feel that they belong to something. They need "identity."

Young girls try to gain a sense of identity in myriad ways: fashions, hairstyles, activities, jewelry, attachments to rock bands, wealth, size of home, family name and heritage, just to name a few. Their sense of identity shapes who they are. It affects their goals and basic belief systems, leading to confidence or insecurity, rest or restlessness, hope or hopelessness.

Thankfully, our daughters' identities do not need to be dependent on such changeable external forces as trends, looks, and personal image. As believers, we hope to communicate that everyone's true identity is based on her position in Christ and on her inner qualities. But convincing a young girl of this reality may not be as easy as it sounds. As moms, we need to be prepared.

Our daughters are uniquely created by God to blossom and grow into beautiful women of His design. These precious flowers are both tender and strong. Some don't know their strength, while others exert it too frequently. The tender side is often hidden with time. How can we water and prune the flowers, expose them to the light, accept and fashion the thorns to display strength and protection, and explore with love all the shades of color in the petals?

Will we do it perfectly? No. Will we make mistakes? Yes. But our daughters are part of God's garden, and He will always guard and protect His own. He knows our finite capabilities, and He promises to give us His wisdom and discernment as we seek

Him with a whole heart. Isn't it amazing that He has entrusted His precious, developing girl children to us?

It is necessary for us to look closely and lovingly at our daughters, to see beyond their youthful charades in order to understand their needs.

A wealthy couple stayed in an exclusive private club in Paris with their two young daughters. One night their oldest daughter showed up at a dinner party—where her parents' friends were present—dressed in black leather and accompanied by a "forbidden" companion. The youngest daughter, looking innocent as a lamb, claimed to be tired and left the party early. Before returning to the hotel, she sneaked off to see a cute "English Prince Charming" she had met in an elevator earlier that day. The parents were very concerned about the overtly disturbed older daughter, and compared her to their "perfect" daughter who was in bed asleep when they arrived at the hotel after midnight.

Both girls were clamoring for the same guidance from Mom and Dad. They simply had different ways of communicating their needs. It eventually came out that the younger daughter was sneaking out regularly and putting herself in compromising positions with various boys. The parents were shocked, but they finally recognized that both girls were crying out in their own ways, "Help me find out who I am!"

We parents are often tempted to fix the crisis situation—whatever it is—*quickly*. Ban the trendy clothes. Impound the CDs. Confiscate the makeup. Provide a crash course in appropriate and inappropriate behavior with the opposite sex. These solutions may be good and necessary, but they will only be temporary unless we deal with one specific core question.

How can we help our daughters answer the question, *who am I?*

In the movie *Titanic*, the leading female character, Rose, has a very predictable life. She was born into wealth with the understanding that she might lose it all if she doesn't marry well. She is expected to use her position in society to protect her family name and carry on her privileged legacy.

Rose appears to know who she is and what is expected of her. Yet inside she sees someone else—someone who doesn't fit her mother's expectations and is crying to get out and away from the cold, overbearing man she is to marry.

Desperate, Rose decides to end her life. Rather than living a lifetime without love or freedom, she will throw herself off the *Titanic* into the icy waters below.

Her suicide plans are halted by a young man named Jack. Afterward, Jack asks Rose why she had tried to jump off the great ship. She responds, "It was everything—my whole world and the people in it, and the inertia of my life plunging ahead, and me powerless to stop it. . . . I was standing in the middle of a crowded room, screaming at the top of my lungs, and no one even looked up."[2]

Jack helps Rose break out of the mold. Later, when the sinking of the *Titanic* frees her of her obligations, she finds the courage and strength to live out the kind of life she was originally designed to live.

With God's help, we won't have to see our daughters make huge mistakes, latch on to the wrong friends, or face tragedy before they learn who they are and how God has uniquely designed them to fill a special place in the world.

Divorce Can Create an Identity Crisis

When our daughters are seeking out who they really are as young women, it's key for Mom to know her own identity. Women can struggle with knowing who they are—and whose they are—in even the most stable of families, but the life-shattering nature of divorce can raise all kinds of questions about identity.

With the fall of my own marriage, my identity changed. No longer was I wife and mother, but now mom/working mom/breadwinner. How would I deal with these changes and still guide my daughters to develop into strong, godly young women?

Many women who find themselves suddenly single try to find a new romantic relationship to create stability, provide companionship, or fill the void of the dream that died. This often leads to developing *false intimacy*.

Psychotherapist Don Carter and his wife, counselor Angie Carter, discuss on their website the dangers of false intimacy:

> False intimacy is often mistaken for true love because it can be intense. . . .
>
> Beneath the waterline of awareness . . . lies the emotional woundedness of abandonment, shame, and contempt.
>
> The abandonment represents the original emotional wounds caused by unmet dependency needs, the shame is an emotional infection that sets in, and the "scab of contempt" represents all of the crusty feelings of anger, bitterness, & resentment that come from having to live this way.[3]

Understanding false intimacy helped me see more clearly how *true* intimacy—the kind that God created for us to experience in marriage—functions. As my daughters have matured, we've talked about what true intimacy looks like because they didn't get to see it modeled in their own home. The temptation of false intimacy is strong, but ultimately it does not allow a woman to stay focused in her own identity in Christ.

I have spoken with women who believe they need to seek divorce and single moms who are dealing with its aftermath. We all agree that God hates divorce. It is never the best option. No matter the reason for the separation, how much support we have, or how bad the situation in the marriage is, divorce is a heartbreaking process. Central to reclaiming our identities is remembering that God has a plan and a purpose for you and for me. It starts when we come before Him humbly to seek forgiveness and grace, asking that God would reveal our own sin and bring healing so the same issues won't be repeated in another marriage. We must live what we tell our girls: It's not about finding the right person; it's about being the right person before God so that we will know whether a relationship is a gift from Him or is a distraction or a temptation. It's about daily walking with Him, hearing His voice, and moment by moment seeking to honor Him first and foremost with our lives.

Discovering and Developing Natural Gifts

Whether mother or daughter, our true identities as women are more clearly defined as we seek God to understand how He created us and for what purpose. Some moms and their girls share similar gifts; other mothers and daughters are gifted in totally different areas. Either way, it's important to note that we are talking about *developing our daughters'* gifts, not our own. We moms are sometimes tempted to blur the boundaries between our girls and ourselves. (More about that later.) Let's be clear up front: we cannot project our own dreams or goals on our daughters. Each girl, young as she may be, has a life of her own to live. It's so easy for us to enroll them in ballet or sign them up for the swim team or teach them French because that is what *we* did. Yes, it's important to expose them to many different activities, but after the exposure, we need to ask two very important questions: Does this activity complement her natural gifts? Is her participation unnatural or forced?

Janie was ten, and she had taken horseback-riding lessons since her third birthday. She enjoyed riding, but what she *really* wanted was to take another gymnastics class. It wasn't that she was fickle—Janie's uncle had had a terrible accident on his horse and was almost killed. This frightened Janie, and she soon learned that all of her other cousins had discontinued their lessons. But Janie's mother was an accomplished rider and wanted her daughter to be the same. She insisted that Janie continue.

If Janie had loved riding, it would have been important for her to learn from the tragedy, to overcome her fear and not to let it keep her from riding. However, this was not the case. Instead, she suffered a great deal of emotional upheaval because her mother insisted that she carry on with her lessons. This mom was convinced that what was good for her was good for Janie too—a classic example of a mother vicariously living out her dreams through her daughter. Mothers who behave this way want to either relive past glories through their daughters or live out a dream that was never fulfilled in their own lives. Bottom line—it's bad for everybody.

God has designed each one of us with a unique purpose in life, and it is essential that we bring up our daughters according to God's plan and purpose. Proverbs 22:6 gives parents a command with a promise: "Train up a child in the way [she] should go, even when [she] is old [she] will not depart from it." We train them through both wisdom and instruction, but the emphasis is on training them in *the ways God has designed for them to walk.* As moms, we quite naturally want the best for our children. Often it's easier for us to encourage them in the areas in which we are comfortable, rather than in seeking their strengths, which can often lead into unfamiliar territory.

What activity seems to make your daughter smile? What motivates her? What causes her to talk excitedly about her efforts? Is it something you are able to share with her, or is it something she's discovered on her own? Take the time to reflect on her likes and dislikes, on what energizes her and what bores her, on what brings out her creative talents and what seems to stifle her. Ask God to help you help her to discover the gifts, talents, and potential He has placed inside your daughter, and try to work wholeheartedly with her to develop them to their fullest potential.

Know Her Natural Personality

The answer to "Who am I?" isn't just found in what our daughters like to do. It's also important for us to know what they are really like on the inside. Is your daughter an introvert or an extrovert? Which would appeal more to her, attending the next party or a chance to curl up with her favorite book? Does she have a quick temper or an easygoing style? Can you describe your daughter's temperament?

No one has done more to help clarify personality temperaments than Tim and Beverly LaHaye. I first met them when they came to our church when I was in junior high school. Later, after my mother began working closely with Beverly on Concerned Women for America, she and I went to Washington, DC, to attend several meetings, and there I was able to spend some time with Beverly. She is a compassionate woman who is deeply committed to Christian causes and to bringing them into public awareness.

Our conversation turned to different personality types, so I posed questions about temperaments and how they relate to relationships. Beverly led me to her office, where she gave me several of the books she and her husband have written on the subject. Our conversation that day helped me see the importance of understanding temperaments, and now that I have children of my own, I often remind myself of their differing styles and characteristics.

Here's one example of how awareness of temperaments can be helpful. Mary was a beautiful and independent child who formed an opinion about everything. At home she was happy and talkative, but in new situations she was very shy. For her true personality to come out, she needed to be very comfortable.

When Mary enrolled in a new school, her mother had to take her to visit the classroom several times so she could feel prepared for the first day of classes. It took Mary a long time to get used to new social situations, and yet at home she could take just about anything in stride. Mary's personality baffled her mother until she discovered the four personality traits: melancholy, choleric, sanguine, and phlegmatic. She was able to see that Mary was a melancholy-choleric child. Outside of the home Mary was very melancholy, but at home the choleric side of her personality shone.

Let's look more closely at each of the four personality traits. See if you can find aspects of your daughter's personality among the following descriptions, bearing in mind that most of us possess combinations of at least two temperaments.

Sanguine

Sally Sanguine is outgoing and fun. She gets invited to everything because she is the life of the party. The room lights up when Sally enters, and she is never at a loss for words. Her stories, although usually embellished, are the most entertaining. She is very generous with her time, talents, and resources, and she shows great compassion to those in need.

People are drawn to Sally's charismatic and enthusiastic personality, yet they become frustrated with her lack of discipline, organization, and follow-through. Her room is usually a mess because her focus is on people. She will quickly become your "new best friend," but she has a hard time fulfilling the promises that she makes in the moment.

Sally's outgoing personality often covers up a fearful and insecure girl, and this emotional instability can surface in unhealthy relationships. Situational ethics tend to rule a Sanguine's heart, so it's important that Sally learn to accept full responsibility for her actions and understand that her weaknesses can be overcome as she learns to walk through life in God's power, not her own.

Choleric

Chloe Choleric is an independent, confident leader who is constantly active. People are drawn to her ability to make decisions and see the big picture. She is a visionary who knows how to motivate people and plan worthwhile projects. She is very determined, optimistic, and decisive. Those who lack these qualities look to Chloe for strength and direction. If she is told, "It can't be done!" that is not a roadblock, but rather a challenge to figure out how to accomplish the impossible . . . and she usually does it successfully!

Because she is very self-sufficient and opinionated, others often feel less important or used in the process of interacting with Chloe. The project seems to be the focus, and friends are often left with hurt feelings. Her anger may not be as explosive as Sally's, but it can be cruel and has a stronger effect on those in its path. While Sally will seek forgiveness, Chloe will tend to see nothing wrong with her actions and proceed to justify them until all opposition gets on her page. The breaking point for a choleric is to recognize and relinquish her pride (which is what precedes a fall). When she realizes that it is not by her might or power that things are accomplished, but only by the Spirit of the Lord, then her gifts can be the most effective.

Melancholy

Molly Melancholy is a very faithful and loyal friend. She is not one to seek out people, but once she lets another person in, she is 100 percent committed. She is gifted and analytical and has a great appreciation for the fine arts. Molly tends to be a perfectionist and is very dependable by nature. In fact, she gets the most satisfaction out of serving others in a way that requires sacrifice on her part. She is extremely emotionally sensitive and thus is more in tune with the needs of others. This sensitivity can also spiral her into a depression and affect her relationships because she has a hard time taking people at face value and is suspicious when someone gives her too much attention. She can become moody and negative, having a hard time getting motivated to overcome obstacles.

Molly is the perfect balance for Chloe because she can see the realistic view and take practical steps forward; however, a spirit of criticism can plague her relationships. This is the greatest obstacle to her growth because when an exciting opportunity is before her, she immediately focuses on all of the potential problems. Melancholy is the most self-centered of the temperaments, so Molly evaluates life in relation to herself. She can be idealistic, and her anger is often stored and then released through making unreasonable decisions. This temperament has the most potential to be used mightily by God when its strengths and weaknesses are brought under God's control. Most of the great Bible characters were Melancholies.

Phlegmatic

Phoebe Phlegmatic is an easygoing and enjoyable girl who always keeps the peace in the family. Everyone likes her, and she is usually volunteered to be the diplomat of the group. She must be encouraged to step up to the plate because she would rather observe life and not get too involved. However, when

Phoebe is placed in a leadership position, she will bring order and harmony, which increase productivity. She is a very gracious and patient person who rarely gets upset.

Phoebe is a great babysitter and may grow up to be a teacher because she notices what really matters in life and wants to help others fulfill their dreams. Her natural dry sense of humor will have people rolling with laughter when she has hardly cracked a smile. Phoebe is a calm, quiet, efficient, and organized girl who tends to be conservative. Her laid-back nature will often prove her to be unmotivated and sluggish when it comes to accomplishing small and large tasks. She can be extremely stubborn and tends to be self-protective. She can also become very indecisive and fearful in decision making. Phoebe needs to find her "motivation button" and then allow God's power and promises to overcome the fear and launch her into a fulfilled life!

This is just a brief overview of the four personalities that have been identified. There are actually twelve blends of these personality traits that fairly well describe most people. Look at the chart on page 16 and try to determine your daughter's primary and secondary traits; then check out your own. I have found that as we grow in our walks with God and learn how to live life through the power of the Holy Spirit, our strengths will develop into a balance of all four temperaments. However, we can also pinpoint our natural personality blend by identifying our weaknesses.

Understanding our daughters' "natural bents" allows us to know how to more effectively communicate with them and assist in answering the "Who am I?" question in a way that penetrates their hearts and directs their lives. But that's still not enough. To give our girls concrete evidence that they are unique and special, one-of-a-kind creations in God's world, let's look at life through God's eyes and the wisdom He gives us in our instruction book for life, the Bible.

Four Personality Types

Extrovert	Extrovert	Introvert	Introvert
Achiever	Communicator	Thinker	Observer
Choleric	Sanguine	Melancholy	Phlegmatic

STRENGTHS

Independent	Talkative	Analytical	Easygoing
Leader	Emotional	Self-sacrificing	Consistent
Charismatic	Optimistic	Dutiful	Witty
Decisive	Sense of humor	Idealistic	Patient
Confident	Enthusiastic	Sensitive	Sympathetic
Goal-oriented	Inspirational	Economical	Mediator
Visionary	Friendly	Faithful	Competent
Delegates	Forgiving	Creative	Agreeable
Productive	Spontaneous	Compassionate	Administrative

WEAKNESSES

Bossy	Compulsive	Negative	Self-righteous
Unemotional	Naive	Self-centered	Unmotivated
Overbearing	Exaggerates	Unforgiving	Judgmental
Controversial	Interrupts	Reluctant	Sarcastic
Manipulative	Fickle	Suspicious	Indifferent
Demanding	Undisciplined	Antagonistic	Lazy
Controlling	Egocentric	Critical	Indecisive
Arrogant	Selfish	Insecure	Irresponsible
"Know-it-all"	Possessive	Perfectionist	Shy

She's Twelve Going on Twenty

Girl Power vs. God Power

People described Diane as cute and fun. On the cheerleading squad she was always the one on top of the pyramid. Then, rather unexpectedly, at age twelve her body started to change. Not only was she maturing, but her metabolism was shifting too. And it wasn't long before she was no longer on top of the pyramid. Unfortunately, Diane's identity was so wrapped up in her petite size that she could not deal with a more shapely body or a few extra pounds. She fell into an eating disorder. She was afraid to let go of who she *thought* she was, so she couldn't become the young lady that God had uniquely created.

When our hearts become hardened to God's growth process—physically, emotionally, or spiritually—it keeps us from becoming all that He designed. He is the Potter; we are the clay. When Diane took her body size into her own hands, it was as if she jumped off the Potter's wheel and said, "I like the way I am, and I don't want to grow up." She could not believe and trust that her Creator saw the whole picture and loved her enough to wisely and carefully mold her into a beautiful, fully developed woman.

The way we live our lives emanates from our belief systems, and our belief systems are determined by our views of God. While the world tries to convince our daughters that "Girl Power" is the secret to their success, our message to them is that to safely venture into an unfamiliar future, they must place their confidence wholeheartedly in their heavenly Father. As moms, we can assist our daughters by assuring them that "God Power" is the real hope for their future. God's power helps us discover who we are and why we are here, and it is increasingly activated as we come to know our Creator intimately.

God created us, so He knows us better than we know ourselves. We often overlook or otherwise fail to see the details of our lives and hearts, but God in His grace and mercy reveals them to us over time. I'm thankful that He does not uncover everything all at once—that would be overwhelming. Instead, all of us—young and old alike—are in a process of discovering who we really are, a process that will take a lifetime.

In Psalm 139, King David beautifully shares how God intimately knows us and intricately created us in His image. Here are some excerpts:

> O LORD, You have searched me and known me . . .
> And are intimately acquainted with all my ways.
> Even before there is a word on my tongue,
> Behold, O LORD, You know it all. . . .
> Where can I go from Your Spirit?
> Or where can I flee from Your presence?
> If I ascend to heaven, You are there . . .
> If I dwell in the remotest part of the sea,
> Even there Your hand will lead me,
> And Your right hand will lay hold of me. . . .
> For You formed my inward parts;
> You wove me in my mother's womb.
> I will give thanks to You, for I am fearfully and wonderfully made. . . .
> My frame was not hidden from You,
> When I was made in secret,
> And skillfully wrought in the depths of the earth;

Your eyes have seen my unformed substance;
And in Your book were all written,
The days that were ordained for me,
When as yet there was not one of them. . . .
Search me, O God, and know my heart;
Try me and know my anxious thoughts;
And see if there be any hurtful way in me,
And lead me in the everlasting way. (vv. 1, 3–4, 7–8,
9–10, 13–16, 23–24)

When Rachel was thirteen, she felt that no one really loved her, especially her mom and dad. She had been adopted at the age of two, and even though her parents said that should make her feel even more special, she wondered why her birth parents didn't want her anymore. One Sunday when she went to church with a friend, the Scripture reading was Psalm 139. She was amazed that God knew so much about her even before she was born. He knew her past and her future. He knew her thoughts and her secrets. Rachel started asking a lot of questions about life and God. Then she realized that she could know Him too. It changed her life.

Today Rachel is a calligraphy artist, and her artfully designed and framed renderings of Psalm 139 are sold in gift shops throughout the world. Rachel's prayer is that God will use that scripture to change others' lives as it has her own.

Have you and your daughter read Psalm 139 together? There is no better way to help her realize that she is uniquely created and uniquely loved by God. As you and your daughter talk together about the big question "Who am I?" you may not find all the answers at once, but together you can ask God to reveal whatever He wants her to know. Don't forget to pray together, and while you're praying, remember to thank God for your daughter's talents, her temperament, and her one-of-a-kind place in His creation.

Moms & Daughters:
Working It Out Together

1. Start a journal that you and your daughter can share.

2. Sit with your daughter and write down all the *external* gifts your daughter may have—good looks, height, family background, financial security, and so on. Help her learn that these are blessings from the Lord and not rights.

3. A few days later, write with her the gifts and talents that help define who she is: abilities for basketball, ballet, and piano; being giving and loving; having a good sense of humor; and so on. Talk about how these areas are currently being nurtured, and ask her to make suggestions about how you can help her grow and develop in these areas. Find out if there are things that she feels pressured to do, and determine whether they are things that she needs to persevere in or if these are areas where you are requiring her to be something that she is not.

4. Discuss the four different personality types and determine which ones describe you and your daughter. Remember that most of us are a combination.

5. Discuss your relationship with God. Does she know and trust her Creator? Try to memorize Psalm 139 together.

Why Am I Here?

Simon Birch is a powerful movie about a little boy who has a birth defect and is not expected to live very long. To everyone's amazement he continues to live, and more than simply surviving, in some way or another, he constantly makes a difference in the lives of the people in his path.

Simon has the wisdom of a twelve-year-old and the physical size of a four-year-old. He and his best friend, Joe, are always exploring the question "Why?" Why can't Simon live a normal life? Why did Joe's beautiful and insightful mother die? Why are we here in the first place?

When the two boys get into trouble, they are required to help out at a church camp. Their bus is in an accident, and Simon ends up saving all the children on the bus, barely getting out alive. At last he knows his purpose and realizes he has fulfilled it. Shortly after the accident, Simon goes to heaven, but not before his brief time on earth teaches Joe that life truly has meaning and purpose.[1]

Many young viewers were deeply moved by the character Simon Birch. I think the movie provided a beautiful reminder that even when adolescents are hurting and life seems futile, there still is hope. A glimpse into someone else's life—especially of someone as special as Simon—instantly diminishes the weight of our own limitations. Most of all, we are assured that God has a beautiful design for every life.

How Does Your Daughter Process the Issues of Life?

At about age nine, a young girl's world starts to shift. She begins to question many aspects of her safe and secure life. Her thoughts and emotions will either be expressed or suppressed, because every child reacts differently. This is why it is so important that, as mothers, we are sensitive to how our little girls are designed. How does your daughter deal with life as it unfolds around her?

One Thanksgiving we traveled to Houston to be with my family. For the first time in five years, all the aunts, uncles, and cousins were there to participate in our twice-a-decade "Morris family photo." But things didn't go as planned. When we arrived, we learned that John, my twenty-four-year-old cousin, had been killed in a motorcycle accident. The holiday was spent comforting the family, especially John's wife of fourteen months, Cristy.

She's Twelve Going on Twenty

I watched my children respond to the unexpected turn of events. Two of them were very vocal. We all had to confront the reality of John's death because they kept asking questions or making definitive statements such as "John died. Everyone is sad, but everyone is happy that he's in heaven with Jesus."

My other two children were very polite but did not say much (the fifth was too little to understand). One of them, along with John's brother, cried a little at first, and then two days later the reality hit, and the tears really began. When we returned home after the funeral, one of our more vocal children went with me to the store and proceeded to explain to the clerk with great detail the account of John's death and the hope that we have in Christ. This experience helped me see more clearly how differently each child reacted to the tragedy.

After observing my own children, and interacting with countless others, I've noticed that there seem to be three different responses to life's challenges, hurts, and issues.

1. The "tell it like it is" kids need us to listen, pose questions, and provide direction. Proverbs is the book of wisdom, and it tells us in chapter 25, verse 11, "Like apples of gold in settings of silver is a word spoken in right circumstances."
2. The "tell me what I'm thinking" kids need us to draw out the thoughts and the longings in their hearts. Proverbs 20:5 says, "A plan in the heart of a young lady is like deep water, but a mom of understanding draws it out" (paraphrase).
3. The "I know what I'm thinking, but what am I feeling?" children need us to let them process the reality

and be available to hold them, to listen, and to share with them whenever they are ready to talk and listen. Proverbs 3:5–6 says, "Trust in the LORD with all your heart, and do not lean on your own understanding. In all your ways acknowledge Him, and He will make your paths straight."

Whatever their personality styles, temperaments, or emotional makeups, both your children and mine need us to pray with them and to be sensitive to their needs in each specific situation. And although it helps us, as moms, to watch for those three possible responses in our daughters, we must remember that our children will often surprise us with an unexpected reaction.

Discovering Your Daughter's Spiritual Gifts

In Psalm 127:3 we are told "Behold, children are a gift of the LORD; the fruit of the womb is a reward." God has given us a beautiful present, a special treasure to love and nurture until adulthood. And within the souls of our daughters, He has placed some incredible gifts. In Romans 12:6–8 we are told, "Since we have gifts that differ according to the grace given to us, each of us is to exercise them accordingly: if prophecy, according to the proportion of his faith; if service, in his serving; or he who teaches, in his teaching; or he who exhorts, in his exhortation; he who gives, with liberality; he who leads, with diligence, he who shows mercy, with cheerfulness."

How can we know which spiritual gifts our daughters

have been given? For that matter, what about our own gifts? I ran across a helpful test for discerning our spiritual gifts. It has been an invaluable asset for our family, assisting us in our efforts to understand one another better, and I've developed a similar inventory, included here. Take a few minutes to go through the test yourself, and help your daughter do the same.

Discerning Your Spiritual Gift

. . . .

In each section below, check the sentences that apply to you. (You may check more than one in each section.)

1. O I often feel insignificant and believe that what other people do is more important than what I do.
   O I have a hard time mending my relationship with anyone who crosses me.
   O I consider myself to be very reflective. I delight in coming up with ideas that are fresh and new.
   O I don't like people to know my business or to "see into" me.
   O I take asset building/protection very seriously.
   O I stick to one thing at a time, and do not like complication. I'm often accused of having tunnel vision.
   O I'm a loner.
   O I think about money a lot.
   O It seems that I am often misunderstood when I speak to others.
   O I take pleasure in making money and in sharing it with charitable causes.

2. ○ I often have ideas, and I enjoy sharing my ideas and opinions with my peers.

   ○ I get incensed or offended if I am opposed or don't get my way.

   ○ It's easy for me to tell if someone has not thought ahead when presenting an idea.

   ○ People accuse me of being a show-off because I take a long time explaining things.

   ○ I relish overseeing complex projects.

   ○ When I talk about something, I believe I see the "big picture."

   ○ I think any task can be done, whether or not it's complex.

   ○ I want to be involved in a lot of things at the same time.

   ○ People often think I care more about finishing an assignment than I do about the people who are helping with it.

   ○ It's hard sometimes to get going on something, even though I enjoy working.

3. ○ I am so focused on the "big stuff" that it's often difficult to get the standard tasks accomplished.

   ○ People sometimes compare me to the "absent-minded professor."

   ○ I have to investigate people's conclusions for myself. Until I have done so, I am suspicious of their rationale or methods.

   ○ I am an intellectual, no doubt about it.

   ○ I love to thoroughly investigate and explore an interesting topic.

   ○ I am more meticulous and precise than other people.

   ○ Most people are too casual in their manner of trying to grasp something, because they aren't very sharp.

○ When I can't get needed information or can't comprehend something, it makes me very exasperated.

○ I go to great lengths to learn the truth about a matter.

○ If someone really wants to learn, I am more than happy to help him understand.

4. ○ I am very philosophical, and I enjoy convincing people to embrace my opinions and theories.

○ I can identify someone with ulterior motives, as well as someone whose motives are genuine.

○ I want to know, *Why, why, why?* . . . about everything.

○ I am certain that there is a sensible and rational way to work out any issue or dilemma.

○ People see me as judgmental, because I am very direct. I'm accused of not having much tact, so I often "ruffle people's feathers."

○ I'm not much into "gray areas." To me, everything's black and white.

○ I don't like jesting very much because it's silly. I don't tell jokes often, and I dislike small talk.

○ I like to be in control.

○ I follow rules to the letter and am very unyielding about it.

○ If there is a conflict between two friends or coworkers, I want them to talk it over right away and resolve the issue.

5. ○ I like working where there is no discord among the workers, and I can be counted on to work hard in such an environment.

○ I can't put up with antagonistic people who are insensitive to the feelings of others.

○ I am told that my explanations are too lengthy.

○ I back off when I'm agitated, rather than making matters worse, because I don't like strife.

○ I'm not comfortable in an environment where there is no order and agreement. I'm also unhappy if there are no friendships among those present, or if the setting is not pleasing to the eye.

○ I try hard not to irritate people when I am explaining something.

○ Integrity and sincerity are important to me in a person.

○ I am perceptive and can identify people's weaknesses in character.

○ I can relate to the feelings of others because I am sensitive.

○ If someone is grieved or distressed, I can read it in her eyes.

6. ○ If the work climate is antagonistic, I'd rather quit than remain on the job.

○ I get fed up with people who are always at war with one another. I don't want to be put in the middle of their gossip about each other.

○ I like for the tasks assigned to me to be of consequence, because I am a good worker.

○ I like to help and satisfy others, especially if my deeds are genuinely appreciated.

○ I like working behind the scenes. I'm uncomfortable in the limelight.

○ I'm good at a lot of things, so I'm often accused of being a jack-of-all-trades. I also tend to overcommit and take on too much responsibility.

O I really like to make lists of procedures, and I always have a "to do" list. I take great pleasure in checking off the items as I complete them, and I like to know the details of every job I do.

O I'd rather not perform a task than to do it wrong. I don't want anyone to be disgruntled with a job done improperly, so I want complete information on how it is to be done.

O I read the instruction manual before trying something new. Once I know how, I rarely forget, and am very inflexible about changing something that already works for me.

7. O I'm a mixture of all of the above things. I think they all apply to me at times.

O I have to see action, and I am bored when nothing is happening.

O Some people think I have an overinflated ego because of my self-confidence.

O If a problem is not actually in the way of getting a job done, then I'd rather ignore it.

O In addition to task completion, it is important for me to see people develop and advance.

O I just don't have time to let obstacles get me off task.

O People sometimes accuse me of using them to complete a project, and they think I forget them when the project is complete.

O If I am working closely with someone on an endeavor, I like to make him or her feel very meaningful.

O I am a good one-on-one motivator. I work well person to person.

O I battle discouragement if it takes too long to achieve some visible results.

What is your spiritual gift? After you've checked all the boxes that apply to you, add up all the boxes you checked in each section. The section with the most boxes checked will identify your primary gift. If two sections share the highest number, the one nearest the bottom of the list is most likely your primary gift. Other high scores are secondary gifts.

The gifts that correspond with the sections above are as follows:

1. Benevolence: Desires to perform kind, charitable acts out of a heart full of generosity.
2. Administration: Attends to the details by the process of managing (for example, taking responsibility for a budget, the family, an office, a government or large institution).
3. Instruction/Teaching: Finds joy through training and developing in others a specific skill set, educational process, or acquired knowledge and understanding.
4. Prophecy: Offers clearly inspired statements of a prophetic nature viewed as a revelation of divine will; often these will be predictions of the future revealed under divine inspiration.
5. Showing compassion: Displays genuine depth of feeling for another person's suffering or troubles, leading to acts of kindness that encourage and benefit the one receiving the outpouring of mercy.
6. Help/Service: Looks for opportunities to serve and help in ways that are a gift to others rather than placing a spotlight on oneself (for example, helping at school or church

She's Twelve Going on Twenty

nursery; assisting the elderly; doing "mundane" tasks at home that bless the family).

7. Exhortation/Persuasion: Strongly encourages someone to move in a positive direction through bold warnings that persuade someone to change her course or confirming affirmations to continue on her path.

• •

My friend Abigail had a great desire to homeschool her children, but when she actually began to do it, she struggled continuously. In the midst of her frustration, she took the spiritual gifts test. She had at least several checks in each area indicating her strengths in leadership and exhortation, but she only had one check in the area of teaching strengths.

This test helped Abigail realistically examine her situation and determine that if she felt God was calling her to teach at home, she needed some support. She and some friends worked out a great system where she taught some subjects and delegated others. The children excelled, and she was able to utilize her natural, God-given gifts.

Usually the hardest and the best lessons learned are the ones that occur when we are trying to become something that we are not. Understanding the gifts God has planted within each of us starts us on the path of being used by God to our fullest potential.

One of the ways our daughters will better understand their purpose on this earth is by discovering their unique constellation of spiritual gifts. It will quickly become clear to them that if God has gifted them in specific ways, He has every intention of using them for His kingdom. And that makes the question "Why am I here?" a lot easier to answer.

Personal Growth Through Setting Goals

In Luke 2:52 Jesus' growth through His preadolescent and adolescent years is outlined: "And Jesus kept increasing in wisdom and stature, and in favor with God and men." This verse gives us a clear model for goal setting in our daughters' lives. As we saw in the previous chapter, some personalities are more goal-oriented than others. But whether it is a natural trait or a learned one, setting goals is always a positive experience for our girls, and it's something we can help them do. Let's break down the four areas of personal growth that we can learn from Jesus.

1. Wisdom—the ability to apply the truth that you know to everyday life. This includes all areas of our lives, but since we will later focus on the spiritual in a different way, let's call this area *intellectual*. The goals in this category focus on developing the mind. Place the goals for grades in school and extracurricular reading (novels, biographies, newspapers, magazines) here. Also, add a practical plan to keep up with current events.

2. Stature—growing physically healthy and strong. Jesus (with the help of His parents) took care of His body. This area will be comprised of a practical plan to keep our daughters' bodies fit through a healthy diet and consistent exercise. This category will be titled the *physical*.

When putting together your goals, it is important to include three areas. The first is aerobic exercise. If your daughter plays a sport, then that could fill this area. If not, work with her to think of an alternative—maybe something you can do together.

The second area is weight resistance. (More about this later.) This can be done with some hand and leg weights at home or at a gym. I know one mother and daughter who go to the gym together three times a week. The mom and daughter walk the track and go through the weights side by side. At first they worked with a trained professional, but now they go at their own pace.

The third and very vital area is a healthy diet. Take an inventory of what you and your daughter eat by writing down everything you eat or drink for two weeks. This will help you discover which eating habits are healthy and which ones are not. Then set up a realistic way of eating healthy as a lifestyle. (There are more practical ideas about diet in later chapters.)

3. Favor with God—having a right relationship with our heavenly Father. This is the foundational area in goal setting. Being equipped for life *spiritually* is the key that unlocks the door of success in the other three categories. How can this goal be accomplished in our lives?

First, do you and your daughter have a personal relationship with almighty God through His Son, Jesus Christ? Grow in your relationship through reading the love letter He has written to you, the Bible. Then spend time talking with Him through prayer, and finally, spend time with other Christians for encouragement and accountability.

Now map out how to practically place these priorities in both of your lives. Read the chapter in Proverbs that goes along with that day of the month. Buy a devotional book you can share together. Praying together with your daughter is essential, but also remember to pray alone. In the words of the Bible, "Pray without ceasing" (1 Thess. 5:17).

Getting together with others to walk or to eat, to pray or to discuss the issues of life is a great opportunity to strengthen yourself spiritually. Whenever possible, include your daughter in everyday spiritual disciplines that will help her learn simply by watching. These are just a few ideas to help us walk forward in life in a way that pleases the Lord.

4. Favor with Man—deals with our interpersonal relationships and involves our goals *socially*. First look at the relationships within your family.

What goals can be set to enhance and grow the way you relate to your husband, your daughter, your other children, and your parents? What about your relatives and your friends? Also, if possible, spend time with a mentor—someone a little farther down the road of life. And return the favor—examine the people God has placed in your life, and see if there is someone you can mentor.

Goal Setting

Seek the Lord, set your sights *high*, and remember that accomplishing even a small part of the goal is a part of growing to the place where God has called you to walk!

Area	3–6 Months	6–12 Months	Long-term
Physical			
Eating Habits			
Exercise			

Area	3–6 Months	6–12 Months	Long-term

Social

Moral Choices

Emotional Growth

Relational
(Parents, teachers,
friends, boyfriends, etc.)

Intellectual

Mental

Financial

Spiritual

God's Word

Prayer

Fellowship

Discipleship

• •

Leave time to enjoy life with your daughter. Have fun with her and laugh a *lot*! Daily time to "hang out" is important.

Stay away from making so many goals and commitments that you don't have time to "smell the flowers" along the way.

Once you and your daughter have reflected on these four sets of goals and have placed them on paper (see pages 36–37), it will help you both to answer more clearly the question "Why am I here?"

The #1 Goal: Allowing God to Complete His Work in Her Life

Paul's letter to the Romans is the thesis of our Christian faith. And in Romans 8:28–29 we find our destiny. It says, "And we know that God causes all things to work together for good to those who love God, to those who are called according to His purpose. For those whom He foreknew, He also predestined to become conformed to the image of His Son, so that He would be the firstborn among many brethren."

The overall goal of our lives is to be conformed to the image of God's Son.

What does this mean for our everyday lives? George Barna conducted a survey to define Americans' purpose for living. Sixty-three percent believed that their purpose was to find enjoyment and personal fulfillment. Eighty-four percent believed that people were basically good.[2] Paige Benton, RUF chaplain at Vanderbilt University, says, "The American dream can now be found in becoming a bunch of good people whose goal in life is to please themselves."[3]

The world defines *success* by whether a girl is attractive, dresses nicely, has a good group of friends, comes from a respected family, and becomes a high achiever. According to this system, who we are and what we do define our purpose rather than our purpose defining what we do and who we are.

Can you imagine what it would be like to be perfect? I have a friend who appears to have a perfect life. She is always dressed fashionably, and her children look as if they just stepped out of a portrait. Her husband is handsome and deeply devoted to his family. All of our mutual friends agree that it would be a dream to "be Barb for a day."

Many people like Barb are self-centered and frustrating because they work so hard to paint this perfect picture, but my friend Barb is genuinely wonderful. She is kind, her kids are well behaved, and she and her husband have a healthy marriage. When you get close it becomes clear that what is on the inside is reflected on the outside. Still, tough times have hit their family. Barb was diagnosed with cancer. In the middle of a wonderful life, life can be hard.

The reason our goal is to be conformed to the image of God's Son is because He was the only human to live a perfect life. The only One to face hard times and not sin. The only One to be tempted and still walk in righteousness. Is there anyone else we would want to emulate?

TV is a powerful "toy." It can be constructive by bringing someone else's world to life and helping us understand how others think, feel, and live. Or it can be destructive by bringing evil into our homes and eating away our time as a family. Recently TV brought a new hero into our home. His name is Chris, and his mother passed AIDS on to him at birth. Doctors said that Chris would live only a few years, but he is still making an impact in his world at eleven years of age. He knows that unless a cure is discovered soon, he will die at a young age.

When asked how he views life and death, Chris answered, "I'm not afraid to die. I know that I will go to a better place to be with God. God won't take me until it's my time. I know that I have a purpose here. It's either to find a cure for AIDS or to make sure that people with and without AIDS become friends. I know that there's a reason I'm still alive."

Chris has the right idea, although a terrible tragedy was involved in his discovery. What does it mean for God to complete His plan in our lives? How will we know if we've fulfilled the plan? I love the reminder that life is not a destination; it's a journey. A journey full of joy and pain, trials and triumphs, laughter, lessons, and tears. How can we prepare our daughters for this journey?

We can start by helping them set goals based on what they believe. The exciting thing about living with a goal in mind is that we have clear direction. And do we know where we will end up? No. One of life's greatest adventures begins when God starts to change our direction, sometimes using one passion to lead us to another greater purpose. That is why it's so important to walk with God. Although we set goals, Proverbs reminds us, "In their hearts humans plan their course, but the LORD establishes their steps" (16:9 NIV).

And what about the outcome? That part is God's job. We are to be faithful in our responsibilities, and we can count on Him to be faithful in His promises.

I was traveling with a group of college students when I heard that Maria von Trapp was scheduled to speak in a nearby European village. Her autobiography had been hard to put down, and it was fascinating to learn about parts of her life that were dramatically different from *The Sound of Music*, which happened to be my favorite movie.

Mrs. von Trapp is one of my heroes because she trusted God when her future was so very uncertain. When we finally had a chance to talk, I was so much in awe of her that later on I could hardly recall what had been said, except for her final words. They were unforgettable and remain a compass in my heart. It is a promise to all of us as we seek to love and nurture our daughters. She smiled radiantly, and in her beautiful, broken Austrian accent, she said, "Stay faithful, my child; stay faithful. God is still working, even when you cannot see!"

Moms & Daughters:
Working It Out Together

1. Review your daughter's gifts and talents listed in chapter 1 and compare them to the results of her Spiritual Gifts test.

2. Explore the Bible together, and write down God's goals for His children. Start with Philippians 1:6; 2; and Colossians.

3. Within those goals, sit down a few days later with your daughter and write down her goals in the areas of intellectual, physical, spiritual, and social development. (See the sample chart on pages 36–37.) As we've seen, the basis for this format is found in Luke 2:52, "And Jesus increased in wisdom and stature, and in favor with God and men" (NKJV).

4. With your daughter, each of you write down, in one sentence, the best answer you can think of, right now, to the question "Why am I here?"

What Do I Believe?

"D o you believe in love at first sight?"
"Do you believe in déjà vu?"
"Do you believe in Santa Claus?"
"Do you believe in the right to abortion?"
"Do you believe in God?"
"What do you believe?"

Before long, this world is going to pose some very challenging and powerful questions to our daughters. In fact, from time to time, every one of us is faced with profound questions of belief. And there are those who spend a lifetime trying to find satisfying answers.

On the 1990s television drama *Chicago Hope*, the leading female doctor's daughter Sarah asked her mother, "Do you believe in heaven?"

Her mother told her that she believed in a spirit and that our bodies are recycled into the earth. She couldn't answer when her daughter responded, "So what happens to the spirit part of us?"

Throughout the show, Sarah continued to raise questions. Finally, at the end she asked her mother, "Is it okay for me to believe something that you don't believe?"

Her mother said, "Of course."

Sarah then replied, "Well, if it's okay with you, I'm going to believe in heaven."[1]

We first voice our beliefs to our daughters when we answer their zillion questions during preschool. And that is just the beginning. In fact, we'd better get ready again, because when our daughters start to approach their teens, the questions will come fast and furious and be far more profound. Some girls may inquire verbally; others will wonder silently but draw their own conclusions from watching us. Our daughters' adolescence will present us with one last opportunity to make sure they are able to think through and articulate for themselves what they believe. Our goal is to help them recognize the solid, foundational truths they will need to build their lives upon.

What She Believes Determines How She Lives

To "believe" means to put our faith, confidence, and trust in something or someone. We give credence to that truth, person, or belief system when we allow it to affect how we live. In the book *Eyewitness to America*, we read an account of how one shop owner reacted during the 1992 Los Angeles riots.

May 1, 2:30 pm, Vermont and Manchester Avenues
A single tear is rolling down the right cheek of Norman Simplest, a burly black man in jeans and a bulletproof vest. He has just returned to his business, Commercial Skypager, to find it looted and burned, despite the spray painted letters that said, "Black Owned."

Simplest and his employees—armed with rifles and semiautomatic guns—had guarded it successfully for two nights, but left when the National Guard arrived. His lament was as much about the Guard's failure as it was about black life in Los Angeles. "All it is is building up our hopes for something," he said. "Always building up our hopes for something, to let us down."[2]

Norman Simplest had put his confidence in the National Guard to defend his business. The very name stood for protection, and Mr. Simplest had every reason to believe that the Guard would do its job, successfully securing the area. In his eyes his protectors had let him down when his shop was destroyed, even though they probably did their best with the resources available. Like most things, the National Guard is limited because it is a human enterprise.

How many times have we believed in something, and later seen our beliefs turned into disappointments? How many times have our daughters believed in us for something, only to find somewhere along the way that we have let them down? And what about our faith in God? Have you ever felt that God has not heard you? Have you secretly suspected that He has completely ignored your prayers?

Of course you and I have been disappointed at times—

everyone has. And for that very reason we must know what we believe, no matter what life may bring our way. In turn, we will then be able to share our faith with our daughters. Our belief system—and theirs—must be built on something solid or it will crumble to dust when put to the test.

In many major bookstores there is a section devoted to books about girls. Publishers have realized that there is a great need for information about adolescent females, and they are more than happy to invest in a relatively untapped market. The basic message of all of these "Girl Power" publications is, "Believe in yourself and you can accomplish anything!"

In the preface of a very eye-opening book about girls, *Reviving Ophelia*, Dr. Mary Pipher states, "We had raised our daughters to be assertive and confident, and they seemed to be insecure and concerned with their femininity."[3]

When our girls are taught to place their confidence in themselves, where do they turn when they run out of answers and their worlds start to fall apart? It is my steadfast conviction that our daughters must believe in *Someone greater than themselves*. As Christian mothers, our first responsibility to our girls is to instill in them a personal and authentic faith in Jesus Christ. When their confidence is placed in Him, they will be able to withstand whatever challenges the world may offer.

Avoiding Naive Choices

In Proverbs 14:15 we read, "The naive believes everything, but the sensible [woman] considers [her] steps." How does this look in today's world?

Susan went over to visit her childhood friend Ellen and met Ellen's two-year-old daughter. At the door Susan and Ellen hugged, and Susan then reached down to hug the little girl.

The two-year-old said, "No, I don't want to hug you!"

Ellen felt terrible, but Susan laughed and said, "Hey, I like a girl who knows what she wants."

That kind of childish confidence is sometimes lost as girls start to mature. As I have talked and worked with young girls, I've found that those who move with solid self-confidence into their teenage years are the ones who are most secure in their relationships with God. In that light, they can make healthy choices. If we want our daughters to be prudent—careful, discreet, and wise—instead of naive, we must guide and instruct them in godly ways that will prepare them for the future. And we need to be wise in the ways we teach them.

One woman who provided me with some very important lessons about godly living was Edith Schaeffer, and one particular lesson was unforgettable. At the age of ten I was in Switzerland for six weeks while my father did business in Europe. We stayed in a chalet in the quaint town of Chessiere, which is nestled between two small villages, Huemoz and Villars. Huemoz was the home of L'Abri, a place where people came from all over the world to study God's Word under the teaching of Dr. Francis Schaeffer.

Dr. and Mrs. Schaeffer lived in the town above us, Villars. It was all along the same winding road, so close that my sister and I could walk from L'Abri to the Schaeffers'. It was there that I first gained a love for studying God's Word. I delighted in going to L'Abri's picturesque wooden chapel with its tall, lofted ceilings. There I joined others in listening to

Dr. Schaeffer answer questions as points of Scripture and the impact of Christianity on culture were scrutinized, discussed, and debated for hours.

Meanwhile, Mrs. Schaeffer hosted women and children in their home a few times a week for Bible study. It amazed me how she could effortlessly—or so it seemed—provide so much food for us. I especially fell in love with her chocolate-covered orange rinds. After I had enjoyed far more than my share of them one morning, she invited me to come back that afternoon and help her make some more. As we worked, she commented, "These are for the other children who also like chocolate-covered oranges."

In the weeks that followed, it took a lot of self-control and consideration for me to limit myself to only two pieces each visit. But today as I look back, I so clearly see her wisdom in not giving me a lecture. Instead, she taught about godly behavior by demonstrating that it took time to make those special treats and that everyone needed to have the opportunity to enjoy them.

Teaching lessons without angry lectures builds our daughters' confidence. And that's so important, because girls who are not confident are rarely prudent. Insecure adolescent girls will either believe everything or they will be skeptical and guarded, unwilling to believe anything.

In Proverbs 14:15, we see the contrast between being naive and being prudent. The prudent young woman carefully considers the information given, processes it, and determines what is true and what is not. The naive girl moves uncertainly, accepting all or nothing and, too often, allowing other people and circumstances to control her responses.

How can our daughters become prudent? By allowing God to guide them. By allowing His Word to give them wisdom. By allowing His strength to be made perfect in their areas of weakness. These are vital life lessons for our girls to learn before they enter their mid to late teens. God has entrusted this training to us, which raises a very important question: Are we putting those principles into action in our own lives? Every moral, social, or ethical decision our daughters make will emanate from their core beliefs. A relationship with God and a life foundation laid upon His Word are the most important gifts we can give to our daughters.

Building a Solid Belief System

What do we believe? How do we teach it to our girls? If we as mothers believe it's essential for our daughters to know their God personally, and for them to be able to verbalize what they believe about Him, then how do we model and encourage them to really believe it from the depths of their own souls?

The foundation for a solid belief system is found in God's Word. Let's look at what the Bible says we are called to believe.

In Exodus 4:5, God instructed Moses to use signs, such as allowing his staff to be turned into a snake and then back into a staff, to convince the Egyptian rulers "that they may believe that the LORD, the God of their fathers, the God of Abraham, the God of Isaac, and the God of Jacob, has appeared to you."

In Numbers 14:11, the Lord admonishes His people by asking Moses, "How long will they not believe in Me, despite all the signs which I have performed in their midst?" Throughout the Old Testament we repeatedly find God's people saying that they believe in Him but failing to demonstrate that belief in their daily lives when times got rough. As one prophet wrote, they "draw near with their words and honor [God] with their lip service, but they remove their hearts far from [God]" (Isa. 29:13).

In the New Testament we are called to more specific beliefs. Matthew 21:21–22 says, "Truly I [Jesus] say to you, if you have faith and do not doubt . . . if you say to this mountain, 'Be taken up and cast into the sea,' it will happen. And all things you ask in prayer, believing, you will receive."

"Oh, really?" your daughter may exclaim after reading this verse, as she thinks about an awesome new car. So a word of warning: If your daughter memorizes this verse without any instruction, soon she may start praying for that car, or for a little attention from the cute boy in French class, or for a brand-new height, weight, and size. It is important for us to teach our daughters that believing in prayer doesn't mean bringing a "wish list" to God. It means, instead, that when we are living in a way that pleases God and is in line with His will for our lives (more on what this means later), then we can fervently pray in faith, expecting answers.

In Mark 5, Jesus responds to a father whose daughter has died. In verse 36, Jesus says, "Do not be afraid any longer, only believe." Jesus healed Jairus's daughter by bringing her back to life. Jesus then asked that the girl be taken care of, and that no one be told. Jesus knew exactly what He believed and was completely focused on carrying out whatever God had called Him to do.

Let's follow His example. Let's put our trust in Him and

expect Him to do the unexpected. Do you really believe that is possible? Does your daughter?

What can we do when we know what we should believe, but just can't seem to follow through? Even worse, what can we do when we believe and have faith, but our daughters don't? How can we handle decisions when faith is under attack and unbelief is winning the battle? Let's look again at Mark, the ninth chapter. Here is an example of a parent who is at a loss about how to deal with his child.

A father brings his mute boy to Jesus. Since childhood, the boy has often been subject to convulsions, even to the point of mortal danger. This distressed father asks if Jesus can do anything for his son. Jesus replies in verse 23, '*If* You can?' All things are possible to him who believes" (emphasis added).

The boy's father then cries out from the bottom of his heart, "I do believe; help my unbelief" (v. 24).

Jesus commanded the deaf and dumb spirit to leave the boy and not to enter him again. After a struggle, the demon came out and the boy was healed. Jesus' disciples had tried to cast out the evil spirit before Jesus arrived, but they could not. Jesus told them in Mark 9:29, "This kind cannot come out by anything but prayer."

Our belief will be strengthened as we cry out to God, pouring out our hearts in rivers of emotional, heartfelt prayer.

Georgia was nine years old, and her parents had no idea how to handle her "episodes." She had a gentle strength that won the hearts of her friends and family. But out of what seemed like a vacuum, she would suddenly change. On those occasions, her kind words turned hateful and her loving gestures became hurtful. Her parents handled this in ways they felt were appropriate, but they finally realized that they needed to find a better solution.

Georgia's parents were able to relate to the father in Mark 9. After much prayer and many talks with their daughter before and after her outbursts (nothing could be done during the episodes), they realized, after reading Mark 9, that prayer and fasting were the only answer. Through prayer Georgia's parents built their faith and believed that God could work a miracle in their daughter's heart and mind.

Today, when an outbreak is about to overwhelm Georgia, these faithful parents pray that the Holy Spirit's power will fill their daughter with peace and self-control. As they believe that God will restore her mind and spirit, the power of God takes hold of a seemingly impossible situation, and Georgia is calmed and quieted. The power of a praying parent cannot be denied. With God, all things are possible.

In Romans 10:9 we are told, "If you confess with your mouth Jesus as Lord, and believe in your heart that God raised Him from the dead, you will be saved." Believing in God means putting our full weight of confidence on Him. It means knowing that He will accomplish His work in our lives and in the lives of our daughters. What we believe about God sets the stage for the future—ours, our daughters', and our families'.

Learning to Rightly Relate to Others

As Christian mothers—and fathers, if we are married to believers—we parents can walk our daughters through the process of discovering God's truth, believing the truth, and living out that truth day by day. Let's not fall into the familiar trap of abdicating to the church youth group or the Christian school our responsibility to train up our daughters in the Lord. These support systems are great, but they cannot replace our Christian parenting role.

A solid belief system is just the beginning. If the way we're living and the choices we're making contradict what we say we believe, then whom do we think we're fooling? In 2 Corinthians 13:5 we read, "Examine yourselves as to whether you are in the faith. Test yourselves. Do you not know yourselves, that Jesus Christ is in you?" (NKJV). Now and then we need to go back and examine ourselves. Believing is only the starting line, for even the "demons also believe, and shudder" (James 2:19). Living out what we believe is an ongoing process—a marathon race that lasts a lifetime.

As we wrestle through questions with our daughters, we need to remember that God is building His foundation in their lives. We are there to guide and protect, but we can't force them to believe. The beliefs that last a lifetime will be those that they appropriate for themselves. As we've already come to realize, what they believe will determine how they will live. Hard as it is, we can't do it for them. But we can love. And we can answer questions. And we can follow the principles of Jesus so they can see how it's done.

Putting Love to Work in the World

God's Word paints such a beautiful picture of what it means to love others. Following its precepts, we find the freedom to extend ourselves to others, to share our resources with those in need, and most of all to learn from the people God places in our lives.

In Ephesians 4:1–3 we are told by the apostle Paul, "Therefore I, the prisoner of the Lord, implore you to walk in a manner worthy of the calling with which you have been called, with all humility and gentleness, with patience, showing tolerance for one another in love, being diligent to preserve the unity of the Spirit in the bond of peace."

We are to love all people and walk through life in a way that brings people together. How does this look in our everyday, twenty-first-century world? Here's one good example: Several parents of fifth-grade girls at a local elementary school joined together because they were concerned about social cliques that were forming in their daughters' class. A letter was sent to all of the parents to discuss this issue with their girls. An anonymous letter was also enclosed. It had been written by one fifth grader who felt that she didn't belong in a group, explaining how it was affecting her life.

At the encouragement of several parents, the school brought in a speaker for a special assembly to discuss this issue with the girls. They followed up with a dialogue about it and came up with solutions in a small group setting. I ran into one of the parents the other day who said that this effort had transformed his daughter's social relationships.

This concerned father told me that once his daughter and her friends realized that nothing could make them better than another person—not clothes, family wealth, your house, friends, boyfriends, *nothing*—they started to reach out and include the other girls who had been left on the social fringes.

"It was so rewarding," he said, smiling, "to watch the girls who felt inferior and left out begin to regain their confidence and poise."

This was a real-life example of Philippians 2:3–4: "Do nothing from selfishness or empty conceit, but with humility of mind regard one another as more important than [yourself]; do not merely look out for your own personal interests, but also for the interests of others."

Just as those fifth graders' parents teamed up to help their children and their children's classmates, it is part of our calling to put our faith in action as we care for others. But a word of warning is in order: When our service to others is based on selfish ambition, it affects even our closest and potentially fulfilling relationships. It's vital to seek integrity as we parent and interact with our family and friends.

Our daughters will definitely pick up on our habits. Having integrity means doing what is right when only God is watching. Our beliefs are defined when integrity is tested. How do we respond to temptation in our lives? How do we act when we're cut off in traffic by a bad driver? When a telemarketer interrupts dinner? When our husbands are thoughtless or careless? When a not-so-nice relative says something insulting? When the washing machine breaks down or the checkbook doesn't balance or the car won't start? It is essential for us to look closely at ourselves because we are teaching our daughters as much through our actions as we are through our words of instruction.

What your daughter believes will remain at the core of who she is and will navigate the course of her entire life. In 1887, the evangelist C. H. Spurgeon commented, "Long ago I ceased to count heads. Truth is usually in the minority in this evil world. I have faith in the Lord Jesus for myself, a faith burned into me as with a hot iron. I thank God, what I believe, I shall believe, even if I believe it alone!"[4]

During these few short years until your little girl becomes an adult, take the time to make sure she isn't walking her faith journey alone. Model the faith for her, and walk with her through the issues of life. In doing so, you will help establish what she believes. And you will enable her to become sure-footed as she learns to walk along some of the precarious pathways that lie just ahead of her.

Moms & Daughters: Working It Out Together

1. Get to know God by . . .
   - reading God's Word together.
   - memorizing God's Word and writing favorite verses in your journal. Here are a few great verses to start with:

     Jeremiah 9:23–24

     Proverbs 3:1–8

     1 John 1:9

     Philippians 2:1–11

     Ephesians 4:25–32

     Romans 8:28–29

   - praying together. Write special prayer requests in your journal and keep a record of when prayers are answered.

- fellowshipping with other believers. Spend time together as a family and encourage your daughter to develop friendships with those who have placed their faith and confidence in Christ.

2. Talk through various real-life scenarios with your daughter involving questions of faith. See how she responds. For example:

  - "What would you do if you had a boyfriend who says he's a Christian and participates in a lot of Christian activities, but then tries to convince you that sex (or drinking, or cheating, or smoking) is okay for you?"
  - "Suppose you have just started in a new school and finally become a part of the 'popular group.' But it's now becoming clear that the girls who were nice to you at first are not included in this group. How will you handle their friendships?"

What Is Faith?

4

Heather stared out the window at the English country-side, which unfolded below her like a green quilt spread across the gentle, rolling hills. She was twelve years old, and this was her first airplane ride alone. She was excited, but a little nervous too. Her mom had flown the first leg of the journey with her to make sure she got safely on the plane from New York City to London. In London she would meet some close family friends, the Thompsons, to help look after their kids as they traveled together throughout the United Kingdom and Europe.

"The Thompsons are so excited about your Christian influence on their children," Heather's mother had told her as they said good-bye, her voice warm with pride.

Heather couldn't help but feel a little uncomfortable with her mom's words. She had never told anyone about the questions that had been floating around in her mind over the last year. Mainly, she wondered why her parents believed that Jesus was the only way to heaven. One of Heather's best friends was Jewish. And another girl in her class said that even though there's only one God, there are many ways to find Him.

Heather had been taught all her life that God loved her and had a wonderful plan for her life. Did He also have a great plan for those who didn't know Jesus? If not, how could God be a God of love? If He died for all, wouldn't He love all?

On the plane, Heather sat by a couple from Thailand. They spoke English well, and in the course of their conversation, Heather learned that they placed their faith in Buddha. Heather asked a lot of questions, trying to compare what she believed with what they thought to be true.

After arriving in London, she continued to think deeply about her questions of faith. Finally the subject came up in one of her conversations with the family. Mr. Thompson told a story about a man who came to a crossroads, not knowing which way to take. There he saw a live man and a dead man.

"Which one would you ask for directions, Heather?" Mr. Thompson asked.

"Well, obviously the live man," she replied, "although if the dead man could talk, he would know about life after death."

"What if the live man had already conquered death and could see the eternal picture?"

Mr. Thompson went on to explain that all the other "ways" to heaven—prophets whose teachings include various systems of religious behavior—have one thing in common: they are dead. Jesus is the only One who has risen from the dead and is alive today.

At twelve, Heather's childlike faith was beginning to be tested. It happens to everyone. It will happen to my daughters and it will happen to yours. Fortunately, Heather got some helpful answers at the right time. All her questions weren't resolved, but at least she wasn't moved away from her faith in Jesus by errant teachings.

Jesus is not a tangible person, but He empowers His children with His Holy Spirit. He lives within us and He speaks to us through His Word, the Bible. Hebrews 4:12–13 says, "The word of God is living and active and sharper than any two-edged sword, and piercing as far as the division of soul and spirit, of both joints and marrow, and able to judge the thoughts and intentions of the heart. And there is no creature hidden from His sight, but all things are open and laid bare to the eyes of Him with whom we have to do."

While the proponents of other "ways" to heaven give an account of what they believe and make promises based on their life's experience and "revelations," Jesus' presence in our lives is very active and life-changing. Ritualistic religion cannot bring us into communion with God, but through Jesus we can have a personal relationship with the living God. A personal relationship with Jesus is the only true foundation stone for a Christian life, a stone that we can help put in place for our daughters.

Help Your Daughter to Define Her Faith

Like Heather, all our girls will continue to question their faith throughout their adolescent years. And it's important for us to remember that asking questions is healthy, and occasional doubts are perfectly normal. Unfortunately, many parents are threatened by their children's queries and feel responsible for their lack of faith. They sometimes imagine that they are being personally rejected when their children challenge their faith.

The truth is, girls and boys who blindly believe in their family's religious system without addressing intellectual and emotional challenges end up feeling insecure about their faith. Even if your daughter seems solid in her beliefs, it's still important to walk through steps that will help her define and confirm what she believes.

Many of us are familiar with the definition of *faith* found in Hebrews 11:1: "Now faith is the assurance of things hoped for, the conviction of things not seen." Faith gives reality and proof to that which is unseen. It is hope brought into action in our lives. And when we see our faith fulfilled in one situation, we find that it is strengthened to face other challenges.

When I was ten, my friend's grandfather, Mr. Jones, was dying of cancer and was told that he had three months to live. I started praying for him every day and told all my friends to pray. Mr. Jones lived for three more years, long enough to see his first grandchild get married. Talk about building our faith! My friends and I saw prayers put into action.

Of course, God does not always heal or prolong life when we pray. And that is the very reason why faith is built on trust in a wise and loving Person, who knows far more than we do, and not a prayer formula. Otherwise, faith would be shattered every time prayers were not answered in the way we think they should be.

Trust means putting our full weight of confidence in something or someone. Every time I sit in a chair, I am trusting that it will do what it was designed to do. Rarely do I test a chair before I sit down. If I had a terrible fall because a chair broke under me, then I might be more cautious.

To trust God completely, one must first believe that God is in control and that He wants all things to work together for our good and His glory. When people feel that God has let them down, they may have a hard time trusting and believing that He has their best in mind in His plan. But a little probing usually reveals that these people didn't have a biblical view of God to begin with. Or that they were able to bounce back after a while. Or that their faith proved strong and healthy, even in the midst of a disappointment. But the chances are that we won't know where are daughters are with their faith unless we ask. That's why we need to take the time to stop, look deep into their eyes, and listen carefully when they talk to us.

I met June Carter Cash and her husband, Johnny, on several occasions during my childhood. They worked closely with Billy Graham, so our families crossed paths frequently. When I was sixteen, an uncle set me up with a cute boy from Galveston who was a longtime family friend. We had a good time together, so I invited him to join my family and me for the opening night of the Billy Graham Crusade in Houston.

This boy's sister and my sister were friends, so they both came along, too, as well as his brother, who was paralyzed and mentally impaired due to a car accident that had taken place a year before. During the crusade, my friend's brother asked if he could go to the front and accept Jesus into his life.

The Cashes were both performing that night. When the crusade meeting ended, we all got together backstage, and June gave me a big hug. Then she turned to my handicapped friend. She kneeled down until she was at his eye level, and spoke intently with him for a while.

Afterward, she stood up and looked at me with tears in her eyes. "He truly understands," she said. "His faith is simple, yet it's already strong."

Seeing her compassion and love for him made a lasting impression on me to do the same. Nothing could be more important than taking the time to get at eye level with our daughters—both figuratively and physically—to intently listen, and to look into their eyes as they talk to us. June didn't miss a thing that night when she talked to that young believer. I pray that you and I won't miss anything either when we talk to our beloved children. That's the only way we'll ever know what kind of promises, lies, and myths the world is offering them, and how they are responding to those offers.

How Does the World Define Faith?

"Believe in yourself."

"You can do anything!"

"Keep faith."

"Nothing is impossible for you."

"Just do it!"

These are popular media messages that our daughters

constantly hear. And they sound kind of Christian at first. But the "Girl Power" message focuses on *self*, not God, as the source of all success. Advocates of this message say, "Put your mind to it and you can accomplish anything." And it can work, at least to a point. For example, many great athletes have reached great heights by believing this philosophy. It is a partial truth.

Two thirteen-year-old girls asked me recently how they would be able to know if it was God's will for them to play basketball. They both have natural athletic ability. First, we agreed that when we walk with the Lord day by day and seek Him wholeheartedly, the decisions we make will be within His will. If we start to take the wrong road, the Holy Spirit will put heaviness on our hearts, which will result in our stepping back and seeing how God is trying to direct us.

But the girls weren't satisfied with that. They went on to ask, "What if we don't make the team we really want to make? Do we keep on pursuing it, or do we accept that it's not God's timing?"

That is a very good question, no matter how old we are. We need to find the balance between pressing on faithfully in what God has called and enabled us to do or using pure human determination to make something happen. The world tells us to do the latter without apology.

Many Christians tend to go to one extreme or the other in the name of faith. One side says, "If God closes a door, then He means no, and that's the end of it." I have counseled girls who are afraid to make any decisions or move forward at all "because it might not be God's will." Their faith is in God, but it is a passive faith. They seem to wallow in mediocrity rather than being used mightily by God, all in the name of being patient and godly.

The other extreme says, "God gave me the vision, I know what He has called me to do, and no matter what, I will move forward. Any obstacles will be seen as spiritual warfare, and I will use all of my contacts and resources to overcome them. Come what may, I will make it happen."

Sometimes we receive God's vision, get God's stamp of approval on it, and then grab the vision back into our own hands.

It's good for us to learn from both extremes, and to come under God's sovereign will. Above all else, God wants us and our daughters to come to Him in complete surrender, allowing Him to bring about His purposes in a powerful way.

In Psalm 139:23–24 we are told, "Search me, O God, and know my heart; try me and know my anxious thoughts; and see if there be any hurtful way in me, and lead me in the everlasting way." As God's instruction book for life, the Bible needs to be consulted diligently and its wise counsel heard and obeyed. In doing so, we can overcome the myths of our present "Girl Power" culture, and live our lives God's way. Then He will direct our paths, give us His peace, and provide the "God Power" we need to sustain our faith.

Talking Openly About Faith Questions

Your daughter's faith may be in the process of being built up. Or it may be teetering on the edge of disbelief. Either way, you may not know what's going on unless you ask. An important conversation with your daughter might begin with your saying, "Has your faith changed in the past few months or years? If so, how has it changed?"

In my dialogues with teenage girls around the country, I receive the most feedback to this query. Often the transition from blindly accepting their parents' faith to making it their own is a scary place to walk. Some girls even wonder if their questions are sinful, or if they are placing their salvation on the line. Here are some questions your daughter may have regarding her faith, and some answers that may be helpful to you as you talk to her.

How do I know that the Bible is true? Josh McDowell is a gifted author and speaker who began his journey as an atheist with the intent of proving that the Bible is false. Through his research he found enough substantial evidence to support the Bible, change his mind, and thus become a believer in Jesus Christ. Here are some facts that led to his conclusion. The Bible

1. was written over a span of 1,600 years.
2. was written by forty-plus authors from all different walks of life.
3. was written in different places at different times.
4. was written on three different continents in three different languages.
5. includes writings on hundreds of controversial subjects.[1]

Josh McDowell later challenged a representative from the Great Books of the Western World to consider ten authors from one walk of life, one generation, place, time, mood, continent, and language and to present them with just one controversial subject. "Would the authors agree?" Josh asked.

The man answered, "No! They would have a conglomeration [of opinions]!" Two days later, he, too, became a Christian.[2] The Bible is the living and active Word of God, and it will not return void.

Is Jesus really the Son of God? Jesus clearly stated that He was not *a* Son of God, but *the* Son of God. The ancient Hebrews believed the true Messiah would be recognized because He would fulfill all the relevant prophecies. The chances of one man masterminding the fulfillment of those complex requirements would be like picking a red marble out of a million black ones. If Jesus' claim to be God's Son was false, He was both a liar and a fool because He went on to die for His claim. Or worse, He was a crazy man with delusions of grandeur. None of these conclusions line up with what even non-Christian Jewish historians say about Jesus.

Josephus, one of the historians from Jesus' time, said,

> Now there was about this time Jesus, a wise man, if it be lawful to call Him a man; for he was a doer of wonderful works, a teacher of such men as receive the truth with pleasure. He drew over to him both many of the Jews, and many of the Gentiles. He was [the] Christ. And when Pilate, at the suggestion of the principal men among us, had condemned him to the cross, those that loved him at the first did not forsake him; for he appeared to them alive again on the third day; as the divine prophets had foretold these and ten thousand other wonderful things concerning him. And the tribe of Christians so named from him, are not extinct at this day![3]

She's Twelve Going on Twenty

What if I believe differently from you and Dad? First, ask your daughter, "*How* do you believe differently? Are you talking about essential issues, like salvation, Christ's divinity, or God's loving nature? Or are you struggling with nonessential issues, like dancing, dress, or dating?"

We should try to find common ground with regard to issues God makes clear in His Word. The other points are matters of personal conviction and opinion in which young women (and young men) should honor their parents and submit to their authority while living under their roof. But having said that, it is not necessarily dishonoring to us as parents when our children disagree with us.

It's very important for us as parents to choose our battles carefully and not to fight and bicker over trivial matters. And if there are major disagreements, more will be accomplished in a spirit of love than in an angry, defensive response.

Is it okay to visit another denomination or type of church? Again, the Ten Commandments call upon children to honor their parents so that their lives will be long on the earth. While living at home, it is important for Christian young people to respect their parents' wishes regarding church attendance. But compromise is always possible. For example, in high school I found a nondenominational church that I really liked and attended on Sunday nights with a friend. I still went with my family to their church on Sunday mornings and Wednesday nights.

If your daughter expresses an interest in visiting a place of worship that is not, in your opinion, truly Christian, ask God for wisdom before you permit or refuse to permit her to go. If she does go, make sure she understands the differences between others' beliefs and yours. Pray for the protection of her spirit while she is there, and talk with her when she returns about what she saw and heard.

What Does It Mean to Have Faith as a Child?

Childlike faith is illustrated in Matthew 18. Jesus says in verses 3–5, "Truly I tell you, unless you change and become like little children, you will never enter the kingdom of heaven. Therefore, whoever takes the lowly posistion of this child is the greatest in the kingdom of heaven. And whoever welcomes one such child like this in my name welcomes me" (NIV).

Children are trusting and open. They are excited about what lies ahead. They are very teachable. But something happens as childhood ends and our daughters enter junior high. Bodies begin to transform. Moods soar and plummet. Hormones ebb and flow. Attitudes flash and darken. Many childlike qualities begin to shift into skepticism, lack of communication, and a general know-it-all point of view. How can faith remain humble and intact in the midst of so many changes?

These are challenging days for mothers and their daughters. But nothing will be too hard for us as long as we remember that God is in control. God's peace will reign when our relationships with Him remain consistent. God's love will rule when we refuse to be offended. God's strength will be given when we humble ourselves. God's wisdom will be available to us when we need it. God's grace will be evident when we love unconditionally—no matter what is said or done.

Moms & Daughters:
Working It Out Together

1. With your daughter, write down her three biggest faith questions and your three biggest faith questions.

2. Help her learn how to look for answers in God's Word.

3. Pray with her, asking for God's wisdom and direction as you seek answers together.

4. Write down her definition of faith and yours.

5

Who Is Influencing Me?

It was Christmastime when Suzy and her family moved from a California suburb to an Iowa farm. The day after the Christmas tree came down, innumerable boxes were piled into a huge cross-country van, sorrowful good-byes were said, and off the family went.

This was a huge change and a tough move for twelve-year-old Suzy, and for a while she cried herself to sleep every night. She deeply missed her friends, she was disoriented by the sudden change in lifestyle, and—worst of all for her—she couldn't believe she might never see her boyfriend again.

The day after Christmas vacation, Suzy attended public school for the first time, and it was even worse than she'd feared. It was obvious that everyone was established in one group of friends or another. It wasn't going to be easy for Suzy to find a place for herself. That night, in the quiet of her room, she cried more tears than ever.

Suzy had attended a Christian school all her life, and she tended to be a little rebellious. After a few days at the Iowa school, some girls started talking to her and attempted to befriend her. They seemed a little wild, which was exciting to Suzy. During that first month at her new school, her friendships within this group began to grow.

Meanwhile, Suzy's family was visiting churches in the area. One night some kids from a local church came to visit. One of the girls, Michelle, instantly hit it off with Suzy. The two of them felt as if they'd known each other forever, and they were soon best friends.

Suzy had accepted Jesus into her life when she was five, but since then she had not grown a lot spiritually. Now she and Michelle started reading the Bible together and memorizing verses. It didn't take Suzy long to begin to notice the difference between Michelle and her friends at school, who were very exclusive and put others down a lot. Michelle, on the other hand, was nice to everyone.

As Suzy started challenging her school friends, it put a strain on her relationship with them. Her growth threatened their beliefs and led to alienation. Suzy's feelings were hurt, and she felt more comfortable being a loner at school. Michelle encouraged her to continue to work on her school friendships but to do it in a positive way. This proved harder than a dare, but Suzy embarked on a mission to understand how to show love and true friendship without setting herself against her friends.

What was happening to Suzy? What caused all these changes

in her young life? A recent Barna poll showed that "Evangelism Is Most Effective Among Kids," as most people come to know Christ before the age of eighteen.[1] Of course, we all know about people who have broken that statistic. But as mothers, we need to see how very important the preteen and early teenage years are to our daughters' spirituality. This is indeed a time during which their hearts will continue to be drawn or hardened.

If your daughter's heart is hardened and she is drawn to unwise influences, pray for a Michelle to come into her life, and seek out wise counsel, together or separately. Peers have such a powerful influence on our daughters. As much as we want to be the ones to help, we are most effective when we give encouragement when our daughters make wise choices, and when we listen and comfort them when their choices lead to heartache. As moms, the more we can trust the Lord and know He is working in our daughters' hearts and lives to draw them close to Him, the more we can find peace in parenting. This peace will speak volumes to our daughters and build trust in the mother-daughter relationship too.

Making Ourselves Available

It's almost a certainty that our daughters will search for spiritual answers during these strategic years. The question is, to whom will they go with their questions? Just because my daughter is not talking about them openly does not mean that spiritual concerns aren't important to her. And maybe your daughter isn't talking to you, either. But if not, to whom *is* she talking? What kind of impact are others having in her life?

It's easy for us as parents to get so caught up in our responsibilities that anything we do for our kids seems like time spent with them. The fact is, for mothers, housework and preparing meals and running errands are no substitute for personal interaction. We have to do it all! We have to get the work done, and we have to spend time listening too. Now, that's a tall order, especially if you're a single mom, but it's well worth the effort.

This became all too apparent to me when one of my daughters asked, "Mom, how come you never spend any time with me?"

I was astonished! From my point of view, my whole life was wrapped up in her and my other children. As I probed, I discovered that even though I was present with her all afternoon after school, and we prayed and talked at bedtime, she still wanted something more. She was longing for uninterrupted hang-out time. I have seen a noted difference in all our children since I started making a personal commitment to this kind of quality time.

One of the primary reasons we need to be present and available to our girls is the conversation that springs up unexpectedly when we are relaxing with them. It is often in this context that questions of spirituality, social discomfort, emotional needs, and physical growth are asked. The rule is, the more intimate and awkward the question, the more relaxed the setting in which it is likely to be spontaneously asked.

Circles of Friends, Spheres of Influence

Whether she admits it or not, just about every young girl wants to be popular and accepted by the "in" crowd, regardless of the social situation, whether it's school, church, camp, or home. For Suzy, this desire was threatened when her school friendships shifted. Because of her spiritual growth, her standards changed, and her friends at school didn't like the way that made them feel.

Meanwhile, Suzy was trying hard to understand what was happening to her as she continued to grow. Not only was her body changing, but her emotions were going wild and her mind was spinning with questions. Life had seemed a lot easier when she didn't care what was right or wrong.

Once she met Michelle, she was no longer free to stretch the boundaries. Instead, her heart was turned heavenward. Sometimes Suzy's mom would find her up past midnight still reading the Bible. Now she heard things, saw things, and responded to things differently than ever before.

Suzy watched as her friends at school created conflicts in order to gain control over other people. She was sad to see them put down fellow students who didn't experiment with smoking, sex, and alcohol. Suzy had tried smoking a few months earlier and had quickly discovered that she was allergic to the smoke. She had sipped a beer and thought it tasted disgusting. And when Joe, the boy she liked, tried to entice her to go under the bleachers at the basketball game, she told him no and said that she had made up her mind to wait until marriage for the kind of thing he had in mind.

Suzy was starting to feel that she'd grown past even some of her Christian friends, and now it was hard to relate to them too. For quite a while she was perplexed, unable to understand her feelings, much less to explain them. But Suzy's mother had been watching and praying for her. One day, when the two of them were sitting quietly at the kitchen table, her mom said, "You know, I'm really proud of you, Suzy. You are growing into a trustworthy Christian young woman, and I'm so happy to see it happen before my eyes."

Suzy stared at her mom in disbelief. "I didn't even think you noticed me that much," she said. "With all the other kids, I thought you were too busy to pay any attention."

Her mom shook her head. "No, I've been praying for you and waiting for an opportunity for us to talk. Tell me what's going on in your life. I know you're really committed to Jesus, but how is that affecting your life at school?"

Suzy could hardly believe she was having that kind of conversation with her mother. And she was surprised at some of the wise insights her mother offered. "You know," she told her daughter, "we are called to be 'in the world and not of it.' The trick is to continue in our worldly relationships, but not to allow them to be spiritual influences or emotional supports. Try to make your inner circle of friends those who agree with you spiritually, those who are headed in the same direction with their lifetime goals."

After that encouragement from her mom, and a time of prayer with her, Suzy gradually began to interact with her school friends in a way that positively influenced them but did not produce alienation. For the first time in her life, she felt she was truly being a light to the world. How did she do it? Whether she realized it or not, Suzy was putting into action *three keys to being a positive influence*:

1. Confidence in Christ
2. Commitment to integrity
3. Consistency

Finding Confidence in Christ

Every mother wants her little girl to be happy. But what does that really mean? I'm a little frustrated with the term *happiness* because it seems to be based on our circumstances—circumstances that change and cannot be controlled. Is earthly happiness really what we are offered in a relationship with the Lord?

When Christ takes control of a person's life, He promises to fill us with His peace, which surpasses all understanding (Phil. 4:7). That peace produces joy, which is a much more valuable state of mind than happiness. Joy is a sense of quiet confidence that comes from believing that God is in control.

Suzy had an easy time making friends and appeared to be a confident girl. But as she grew in her faith, she was able to see that she had really been covering up a lot of insecurity. Even though she felt that she was in control and not giving in to peer pressure, she now realized that her self-assurance was based on her ability to fit in with the group.

It was a new experience to no longer be "self-confident," but to allow God's control of her life to be her confidence. Instead of worrying about other people's opinions, whether they laughed at her and why they sometimes didn't accept her, Suzy focused on Christ. She kept reminding herself that her worth was in Him, not in what others thought about her. Even so, the change was scary.

Little by little, her spirit remained at rest even when her emotions were running wild. And after a while, her friends started to accept her just the way she was and to respect her strength in God. Although they were not really "soul mates," they were still friends. And in later years they came to her with questions because it was clear that she had a confidence and a peace of mind that they simply could not copy.

Building up our daughters' confidence is important. We need to avoid insults, criticisms, jokes, or labels that can erode their fragile view of themselves. Sincere compliments are treasures to young girls, and our genuine belief in them will mean more than we can possibly imagine. But teaching our girls to put their confidence in Jesus is the best advice we can give them. A clear awareness of His love, His guidance, His delight in them, His forgiveness, and His good plans for them can make the difficult adolescent years pass with the least possible insecurity, fear, and self-doubt.

Becoming Committed to Integrity

It bears repeating: having integrity means doing what is right when only God is watching. Suzy was trying to grasp this idea and translate it into her life. One of her friends, Halle, seemed to do the right thing no matter what, but it had a lot to do with her fear of getting punished if she didn't. When Halle made mistakes, she felt so ashamed and guilty that it affected every area of her life. Suzy saw her as someone who lived life with integrity, but for the wrong reasons.

"How can we develop real integrity?" she asked her mother one day. "What does it mean? My friend Halle has integrity, but I think it's because she's scared of both God and her parents. On the other hand, sometimes I feel almost free to do wrong things because I know God will forgive me. Where's the balance?"

Suzy's mom studied her daughter's solemn face and smiled. "Hold on a minute," she said, going into her bedroom and returning with her Bible. "Romans 5 and 6 have a lot of important things to say about grace, sin, the Law, freedom, and integrity. Romans 5:20–21 says, 'The Law came in so that the transgression would increase; but where sin increased, grace abounded all the more, so that, as sin reigned in death, even so grace would reign through righteousness to eternal life through Jesus Christ our Lord.' Grace is the answer to Halle's guilt, and it's also the safety net for you. But let's go on to chapter 6."

Suzy's mother continued to read: "'What shall we say then? Are we to continue in sin so that grace may increase? May it never be! How shall we who died to sin still live in it?' So, grace brings freedom from guilt, but does not allow for a license to sin. 'But thanks be to God that though you were slaves of sin, you became obedient *from the heart* to that form of teaching to which you were committed, and having been freed from sin, you became slaves of righteousness. . . . But now having been freed from sin and enslaved to God, you derive your benefit, resulting in sanctification, and the outcome, eternal life. For the wages of sin is death, but the free gift of God is eternal life in Christ Jesus our Lord'" (6:1–2, 17–18, 22–23).

As Suzy's mother helped her understand these scriptures, Suzy found that the key to personal integrity is found in doing what is right from the heart, not for other reasons. Later on, she talked to Halle too. "You know what, Halle? You can never do anything to make God love you any more or any less. Did you know that?"

Suzy began to understand that no matter how much she

tried to do right in the eyes of others, even her parents, she could not please everyone. God is the only One who loves perfectly. And He desires for us—and for our daughters—to have the freedom to live within the boundaries of His truths, which are laid out in His Word.

Accountability

Who has your daughter's ear? What kind of influence are they having in her life? Michelle became a valuable and positive friend in Suzy's life. In Colossians 4:12, Paul wrote about a dear friend: "Epaphras, who is one of your number, a bond-slave of Jesus Christ, sends you his greetings, always laboring earnestly for you in his prayers, that you may stand perfect and fully assured in all the will of God."

Michelle was an Epaphras to Suzy. She was a peer whose mind was tuned in to Suzy's world. She was a trustworthy friend with whom Suzy could be honest about her struggles. Often Michelle encouraged Suzy to talk with her mom about how to deal with a certain situation. And the more Suzy opened up with her mom, the more freedom she was given at home, because trust was being built. Between her mom, Michelle, and other Christian friends, Suzy was able to work through the challenges she faced with her friends at school. A couple of Suzy's classmates even started accompanying Suzy to church.

In 1999, the Littleton, Colorado, school shootings sent a jolt through our country, as have numerous similar incidents in the years since. The front of *Newsweek* in the May 3, 1999, issue boldly asked, "WHY?" What causes teens to kill? Why would they go to such extremes? Psychologist James Garbarino of Cornell University found that "a baby who is unreactive to hugs and smiles can be left to go her natural, antisocial way if frustrated parents become exasperated, withdrawn, neglectful or enraged."[2] Luke Woodham, who murdered three students at age sixteen, said, "My whole life I felt outcasted, alone."[3] So do a lot of adolescents.

A sense of injustice is often accompanied by a feeling of abject powerlessness. One killer profiled in the *Newsweek* piece admitted, "I'd rather be wanted for murder than not wanted at all."[4]

We learned some important lessons from Dylan Klebold and Eric Harris, who committed the Littleton, Colorado, murders. It was not just important that they had friends, but they needed friends who could be a positive influence in their lives. They needed far more than roofs over their heads, food in the refrigerator, and money to spend however they wanted. They needed parents who knew them, cared about them, talked to them, and never gave up on them. They needed to be accountable to others who loved them. And they needed to be accountable to God.

How can we help our daughters through the changes the adolescent years will bring their way? The best we can offer them is our love, our prayers, and our commitment to God's Word and God's ways. Growth brings change, change brings stress, and stress can bring turmoil into a young girl's life. Change also often redirects friendships and influences. As we stay in tune with what our daughters are focusing on and what they talk about every day, we have the chance to influence them. Listening and observing become beacons to inform us how the waves of change are affecting our daughters and how our daughters are affecting their friends. Paying close attention to our girls provides an opportunity for moms to guide the direction of change by wrapping it in a warm blanket of caring and sharing, with the hope that our daughters will be able to welcome it with open arms.

Moms & Daughters:
Working It Out Together

1. With your daughter, write in your journal the stories of your personal relationships with God. How did they begin? What kinds of changes has God made in each of your lives? How have you grown in grace?

2. Write down what you feel your confidence is in, and have her do the same. Discuss confidence in Christ.

3. Define *integrity* and talk about what that means in everyday life. Whom does your daughter think of when she thinks of the word *integrity*? Whom do you think of?

4. Talk about her closest friends. What kind of influence do they have in her life, and how does she influence them?

6

How Can I Feed My Spirit?

You know what? If I don't ask Jesus into my heart, then He won't be my friend." I was just five years old when I informed my mother of a very important lesson I'd learned in my vacation Bible school class.

Mom, who quickly understood that I was ready to accept Jesus as my Savior, smiled and asked, "Well, would you like to invite Jesus into your life?"

"Yes, I would," I answered, nodding emphatically. And with that she explained the gospel to me in terms I could understand, and we prayed together that Jesus would forgive my sins and come into my heart.

Young as I was, from that time on I talked to God all the time and faithfully went to Sunday school. My little friends knew that I was a Christian, and I sometimes told them how they could know Jesus too. God was a regular part of my life, but mostly I focused on things little girls enjoy.

Years passed, and by the time I was eleven or twelve, life started to change. Girls of this age all feel the differences in their bodies, interests, attitudes, and moods and are beginning to realize that they need to strengthen themselves spiritually in order to face the years that lie ahead.

One Sunday night our youth pastor explained to us that there are four ways to make sure we are always growing in our Christian lives. "Never forget the importance of reading God's Word, taking time for prayer, participating in Christian fellowship, and being involved in discipleship. These four things will keep your faith strong and healthy."

As I listened to his words, I realized that besides attending church, hanging out with a few Christian friends, and being present during family devotions, I really wasn't doing any of the things he was suggesting. But because of his challenge and my mom's faithful guidance, I was led into a growing walk with God.

As my own daughters have grown older, I have shared those four principles with them. I hope you'll share them with your girls too. Let's reflect upon them together and see how we can make them a practical part of our families' everyday lives. And since, as mothers, we know that example is the greatest teacher, let's welcome these four disciplines into our own lives too.

Developing a Love for God's Word

Like most kids, I had a lot of questions as a child. Many times, Mom would say, "That's a good question. Let's go to our instruction book for life and see what it says." As I entered junior high, it was easy to become frustrated with the truth when it didn't support my point of view. Usually I was successful in turning my argument into the only logical conclusion. This I had learned from my mother, a brilliant attorney who has never lost a case.

However, it didn't take me long to realize that I could not argue with God's Word. Even today, when my heart wants to take a different path, God's Word holds up a standard I cannot ignore. But we can't make God's Word our standard if we don't know what it says. It must be planted in our hearts and allowed to take root in our lives.

My grandmother's motto is, "Read a proverb a day. There is one for every day of the month!" So, at age twelve, I started reading a proverb, one chapter from the Old Testament, and one chapter from the New Testament every day. With homework and early mornings, it was hard to find the time, but two things helped me. One was a wise word from an older friend challenging me to consistently take some time to read my Bible before studying. It even brought more focus to the study time. The other was reminding myself to carry a pocket Bible in my purse or backpack to provide opportunity for reading throughout the day. As parents, we also get to look for chances to incorporate reading the Word into our children's lives by having family devotions whenever it works. At our house it usually happens during a meal.

Jacqueline's parents had been saving for years to buy her a car when she turned sixteen, but they wanted her to feel she had earned it so she would appreciate the privilege. They decided that if she memorized all of the book of Psalms, they would buy her a car. Jacqueline eagerly wrote out each psalm on a separate index card and carried them with her everywhere. She made it through Psalm 119 just before her sixteenth birthday, and her parents gladly gave her the car when she promised to finish memorizing the rest of the book.

It took another year to learn the last thirty-one psalms because life got busy and she had a lot of places to drive. Still, by the time Jacqueline left for college, she had all the psalms written in her heart. An incentive for memorizing Scripture is an effective motivator, especially with teenagers. Jacqueline's efforts were an unforeseen blessing once she went away to college and faced the spiritual challenges there. And when she was confronted by a personal tragedy at the age of twenty-two, God's Word sustained her. As we teach our daughters the incomparable value of God's Word, we can stand on His promise in Isaiah 55:11: "My word . . . shall not return to Me void, but it shall accomplish what I please" (NKJV).

Discovering the Power of Prayer

"I know that I'm supposed to pray, but when do I pray?" Miki asked me, a slight frown wrinkling her forehead. She was thirteen and couldn't quite figure out how to have a healthy prayer life. "In the morning I barely make it to school on time, no matter when I wake up, and at night I fall asleep reading the Bible. I'm doing something every minute of the day. When am I supposed to pray?"

I love what Paul says in 1 Thessalonians 5:17: "Pray

without ceasing." Prayer can be a quiet, focused time at a particular hour of the day, or it can be an ongoing conversation during our everyday lives. The important point of prayer isn't when or how; it is whether we are communicating with God. It's amazing to think that we can talk openly, anytime, and anywhere with almighty God. He loves us immeasurably and cares about every detail of our lives.

Jesus taught that prayer is supposed to be done in secret, not for the purpose of being noticed by men (Matt. 6:5–7); however, this does not mean we shouldn't pray in public. I had a college friend who did not pray in restaurants because other people might notice. This is not the point of the passage. God always looks at the intention of the heart. If you pray at home before each meal, then you needn't change your habit in public. On the other hand, if you don't usually pray at home and you spot your pastor at a nearby table, don't show off by blessing the food for his benefit.

My friend Mary and I talk all the time. When we don't talk, I miss her and there is a void in my life. We don't have to schedule a time to talk because it's something that naturally happens. This is how it can be with God. Prayer is talking to God. And it's even easier than talking to our friends, because we don't need a phone to call Him. He is always there.

Sometimes my kids tell me, "I want to pray, but I don't know what to say." Maybe your daughter has said the same thing to you. Jesus has given us a beautiful model for prayer in Matthew 6:9–13. He says, "Pray, then, in this way:

"*'Our Father who is in heaven, hallowed be Your name.'*" This shows a spirit of worship and allegiance to God.

"*'Your kingdom come. Your will be done, on earth as it*

is in heaven.'" We should always pray in submission to God's will for our lives.

"'Give us this day our daily bread.'" Jesus wants us to bring our requests before God and to be thankful when He daily provides for our needs.

"'And forgive us our debts, as we also have forgiven our debtors.'" Confession of sin, asking forgiveness for ourselves, and forgiving others are vital aspects of prayer.

"'And do not lead us into temptation, but deliver us from evil.'" In prayer we can seek protection from temptation and deliverance from sin.

"'For Yours is the kingdom and the power and the glory forever. Amen.'" Our prayer ends as it began, in worship and adoration of our heavenly Father.

If you aren't doing so already, now might be a good time to start praying with your daughter. Keep in mind that there is not a right or wrong way to pray. Just pray honestly to the Lord from your heart.

Intercession for others is also an important type of prayer. When our friends or family members are sick, in trouble, facing personal challenges, or otherwise in need of God's touch, we can bring them into His presence and seek His help for them. We can touch them with our prayers even when they are physically far away. Sometimes people say, "Please pray for me!" It's wonderful to remember to do so. But when I was young, I always felt guilty when I promised to pray for someone and then forgot.

Vonette Bright and her late husband, Bill Bright, are the founders of Campus Crusade for Christ and good friends of our family. Vonette has a gift, as did her husband, for sharing

God's vision in a way that ignites spiritual fire in the hearts of others. The first time I received one of Vonette's handwritten letters of encouragement, I noticed that she had written at the end, "I will pray for you as the Lord reminds me." At the time, I was struggling with telling people I would pray for them and later realizing that I hadn't prayed even once. Vonette's statement came as a relief to me; it was an honest way to commit myself to lifting someone up to the Lord.

Forming Christian Friendships

As we discussed in the previous chapter, the leading influencers in your daughter's life, the group toward which your daughter gravitates, will be your biggest clue about where her heart is directed. Proverbs 13:20 says that "he who walks with wise men will be wise, but the companion of fools will suffer harm." Spending time with other Christian kids will bring growth to her life. The opposite is true if she chooses friends who are caught up in the popular culture that surrounds them. But making friends—even Christian friends—is sometimes easier said than done.

For six years I discipled a girl named Julie. She was beautiful and bright, had a loving family, but was extremely insecure when it came to friendships. Just the thought of making new friends overwhelmed her. It was almost impossible for her to try.

Her difficulties were frustrating to me because I couldn't relate to her struggle. I tried to encourage her but soon realized that I was trying to get her to handle things my way, not hers. None of my little tricks worked for her. She wanted friends, I wanted to help her, but we couldn't figure out what she should do.

After two years she finally opened up and said she wanted my help. She was tired of always being on the outside of the crowd. Her biggest hurdle was her height. She looked like a high school student even though she was still in junior high. "I just feel geeky and awkward," she moaned. Some of her peers were Christians, but even so, they could be insensitive and cruel.

Finally, a few other moms and I put together some "girl talks" about friendships and reaching out, and little by little the talks began to have an impact. Julie started becoming more confident in her walk with the Lord and in believing that her worth was found in Him. By her junior year of high school, she was editor of the school newspaper. She had found a fun group of friends who loved one another. Now she's working for a newspaper as a writer in a major city. She is tall, bright, and beautiful. She no longer feels awkward and insecure.

Then there was Jessica. Friendships were her life. She knew how to make them and she knew how to break them. The challenge with Jessica was to help her see all people as valuable whether they were popular or not.

Positive friendships are not always found by being a part of the "in" crowd. Christian fellowship means spending time with people of substance who are not afraid to tell us the truth. Honest friendships aren't easy to find. Jessica needed to face up to the realities of some unhealthy friendships and then give priority to those who would build her up and not pull her down. This transition was tough for her, but as she grew in her walk with the Lord, she started to move toward girls who believed as she did, and to move away from those who didn't have the same value system.

Jessica's mom was a true ally in this process. She was very careful not to alienate Jessy from the girls who seemed to have a negative influence on her daughter. Instead, she often invited them over to their house, along with the girls who were a positive influence.

Her mom also planned social get-togethers with the families of the girls she hoped Jessica would connect with, so they could develop a bond outside of school and church. Through Jessica's mom I have learned a lot of practical ways to influence my children. Friendships deeply affect our children's lives, and as mothers it's crucial that we prayerfully watch over our daughters' friendships in a way that will be both constructive and noncontrolling.

Becoming Disciples and Disciplers

In Titus 2:3–4 Paul instructs older women to teach younger women. His words are aimed at young wives and mothers, but I will never forget my mother telling me when I was twelve that everyone is an "older woman" to someone. Discipling can begin the minute the Lord enters our lives, regardless of our age.

Not long after I graduated from college, a girl in her thirties who was a new Christian asked me to disciple her since she wasn't familiar with the Bible. I felt a little uneasy about her request because I was younger than she was, but the woman who discipled me said, "Don't look at it that way—physical age is not the issue. Instead we need to think about how old we are in the Lord." As it turned out, my friendship with that new believer was a wonderful experience for me. I learned a lot of life lessons from her because she had lived longer than I had, and I was able to help her grow spiritually.

At twelve years of age, I started to be discipled and to grow spiritually. By the time I reached high school, I was able to start discipling some junior high school girls. It was a great time of growth for both them and me. This process put me in a position of great accountability as far as my boyfriend and I were concerned. As I talked to younger girls about what a relationship with integrity should look like, it reminded me that I could do nothing less than hold on to the same standard myself.

Sad as it is, many young girls are in counseling these days because they don't feel that anyone will listen to them, especially their parents. As Christian mothers, let us never forget that our children are our ultimate discipleship responsibility.

Except for times when my own children required my full attention, I have always worked with a group of girls. I meet with them once a week for Bible study and prayer; then we do something social together, such as having lunch at their school, attending a football game, or shopping on the weekend. We also enjoy some one-on-one conversations on the phone during the week.

Discipleship requires a commitment of time, energy, and love, but like motherhood, it is wonderfully rewarding. As moms, we need to disciple our daughters ourselves first. Then as they grow, we can encourage them to disciple someone else. And we can—and should—pray for an "older woman" to come into our daughters' lives to reinforce the commitments we are trying to build into their characters: commitment to

God's Word, to prayer, to solid Christian social connections, and to looking after one another in Christ.

Honoring God Through Our Lives

As I had coffee one morning with a close friend, the conversation turned to what it means to truly honor the Lord. *Honor* is defined as "high respect," "esteem," or "to hold in high regard." We are called in the Ten Commandments to honor our parents so that our lives may be long on the earth (Ex. 20:12). Throughout the Scriptures, we are also called to honor the Lord with our whole hearts. So how do we show honor? How do we know if it's real?

Have you read Psalm 119 lately? It continuously speaks of walking blamelessly before the Lord, seeking Him with a whole heart, and treasuring His Word. It's a lot to live up to. But the final verse says,

> I have gone astray like a lost sheep; seek Your servant,
> For I do not forget Your commandments. (v. 176)

When we go astray, *He seeks us*! Remember His commandments, hide them in your heart, and trust that God will keep you from going astray. This is how we honor God.

As our discussion deepened, I began to see that when we honor God with our very messy and real lives, our kids will honor God, themselves, and others. If we show honor to our children, they will show honor to each other and to us. (Always? I wish!)

We are sinners in desperate need of God's guidance and grace. So do we wallow in the muck between sin and grace to stay dependent on God? As Romans 6:2 says, "May it never be! How shall we who died to sin still live in it?" We are dead to sin, but alive to God. Whether we are twelve, twenty, fifty, or in between, we are daughters of the living God, living under grace with a daily, minute-by-minute dependency on God, who promises to live through us when we honor Him and abandon our lives completely to His will.

Moms & Daughters:
Working It Out Together

1. Develop with your daughter a plan for both of you to memorize Scripture together.

2. Make a list of people you care about, and pray for them together. Be sure to keep track of answers to those prayers.

3. Talk with your daughter about her friends—whom she likes best and why. Let her know how you feel about her friends, and then ask her what she thinks about your friends. You may gain some interesting insights from her.

4. Pray together that God will lead each of you to older women who can disciple you, and to younger Christians you can disciple.

Soul

The soul is our emotional and moral nature. It is the thinking and feeling part of our being that defines who we are and what we believe, and it shapes the people we become. The soul is often overlooked, especially when the body is functioning in a fairly normal manner and good spiritual habits have been established.

The questions, fears, and longings of the soul can become suppressed until signs of health start to visibly break down. This is the most important area for mothers to understand, address with our daughters, and face in ourselves. When God's Spirit has secured the soul, then hidden areas can be explored without fear. Knowing what is deep within the soul provides us and our daughters with the freedom to blossom into the unique women that God has designed.

Family and Friends

Kathy Peel is a gifted speaker and an accomplished author. She is best known for her Family Manager book series. I first saw one of Kathy's books at a local bookstore. One glance at the witty cover and I caught a glimpse of her sense of humor. As I laughed a bit, the bookstore owner mentioned that Kathy had just moved to Nashville from Dallas and was now attending our church.

A few weeks later, through mutual friends, Kathy and I met. The first thing we did was talk and talk about Texas—that's what Texans tend to do. Her bright smile and contagious personality were delightful, and a fun friendship began.

We met in a season when I had four young children and one on the way, a traveling husband, and a home to keep up, and sometimes life seemed overwhelming to me. I've often thought I'd be better at running a corporation than a family. Of course it's fun to be with the kids, but trying to keep all of it together is harder than it seems. Kathy came into my life at a very crucial time. I was pregnant with Mary Morris, my fifth child; in addition, I was writing a book and producing two videos for moms. At the same time Kathy was working on the Family Manager series.

As we sat at an outdoor café, eating our salads and drinking our bottled water, she shared with me the theme of her book. Then she said something that really lifted my spirits. "Kim, you are a family manager," she told me. "Just as a CEO runs a company, you are running your little corporation called the family. Take the God-given skills that you have to run a business and apply them to your home."

Kathy Peel emphasized the importance of making a plan with the family and then working together as a team. She suggested tactics such as offering bonuses and incentives, having picnics, calling family meetings, and learning how to work well together. She also made some great suggestions about maintaining healthy habits when running our homes. The family under my roof is still learning, and I take one day at a time. I am forever grateful for the practical ways she has helped me utilize my gifts to run a more efficient and more loving home.

The Training Ground for Life

Home and family are the settings where we reveal who we really are deep inside, where our strengths and our weaknesses are fully evident. For our children, the home is the training ground for life. When our girls approach age nine, their roles in the home begin to change. No longer are they little children. Instead, they are growing into young ladies with new responsibilities, new perspectives, and new attitudes. They soon discover a different kind of dynamic in their family relationships.

How can parents provide a home that nurtures growth and exploration in a healthy and stable environment? When my first child was born, Josh McDowell told me something that has made a significant difference in our home. "Rules without relationship lead to rebellion," he said. Regardless of the marital status of the parents, whether children live with Mom and Dad, Mom, Dad, one parent and a stepparent, grandparents, or a caring foster family, it's imperative that a wholesome and loving relationship between the children and the adults be maintained. Relationship is everything.

Jody was a terrific girl. She always earned good grades and had a nice group of friends. Her parents divorced when she was eleven, and Jody moved in with her sixty-five-year-old grandmother, who was not in great health. Jody's life drastically changed. Her grandmother slept a lot, so Jody did not have transportation to after-school activities.

It wasn't long before Jody began to have some emotional problems and started lying to get attention. She learned to manipulate to get her own way, and she found ways to stay in control. These traits have stayed with her for years. Her grandmother did the best she could, but she did not build a relationship that supported Jody through her vital adolescent years. When our kids are "acting out" in an unhealthy way, they are probably telling us that there is a breakdown in our relationships with them.

Mothers really are the "CEOs" of their families. But they are more—Mom is the heartbeat of the home. If she is hurting, the children feel it. If she is fulfilled, the children will reflect that too. And if Mom cares, her daughters know it. Every young girl's heart cry is to be understood. Our girls desperately need for us to listen and to care about what they're feeling. As I have interviewed girls around the country, I've asked them about their relationships with their moms. Here's what some of them say:

"I love my mom because I can talk to her and she listens." —Amanda, 16

"Mom, you are all I have. I know how much you've had to go through for my sister and me. How much you've lost so we could gain. Thank you!"—Kristy, 15

"Mom, I'm dealing with premarital sex. I don't know how to tell you. I don't feel close to you because a divorce and a moral lie have pulled us apart."—Jess, 16

"I'm close to my mom because she is open with me and shares her feelings. We get in fights, but we always love each other and work it out. I'm worried about telling her that I have a boyfriend. What will she think of me?"—Mary, 14

"My mom is a great role model for me and she loves me. I wonder if she knows how important she is to me?"—Halle, 13

Our girls will grow up either wanting to emulate us or to be as different from us as possible. And, of course, personality comes into play.

Joanne had two daughters. Tara was a replica of Joanne, while Kara was just like her grandmother—her dad's mom—whom Joanne didn't especially like. Joanne and Tara did everything together. They loved to talk, dress up, and go on outings. Kara sometimes joined them, and Joanne tried to focus on doing things that Kara enjoyed. Still, Kara felt that her mother loved Tara more. Tara grew up to be just like her beautiful, slender mom, while Kara is obese and emotionally unhealthy, which is also due to an abusive father.

What can we do as mothers to win the hearts of our girls?

We can listen. We can stop criticizing, controlling, and complaining. We can speak words of love and encouragement. We can take time to "hang out." We can ask our daughters for their opinions and respect their points of view. We can overlook the things about them that we don't like. We can compliment. We can pray together. We can share hurts and heartaches and hopes and happiness. We can laugh together. We can cry together. We can find common ground and build a relationship from the ground up.

Sometimes, in a culture that preaches self-gratification, we have a hard time setting aside our plans, opinions, and ambitions for the sakes of our children. If only we could realize how quickly childhood passes. How short is the time between babyhood and high school graduation, and how precious is every moment of our child's time with us. Have you ever wondered what your daughter will remember most about you when she's grown up? What words have you said that she will never forget? What memories of you will she take with her when she moves into her college dorm, or settles down in her first apartment, or leaves on her honeymoon?

Bringing up a girl is a family affair. In these last years of childhood, before our daughters' peers become their primary source of influence, we have a brief window of opportunity within the family context to introduce them to life's most important values, principles, and beliefs. Let's try to remember to teach them by asking questions, by listening, and by avoiding lectures and tirades. And let's include their fathers in every way possible—whether we are married to them or working together with them as single parents. Just as girls need a loving, caring mom, they also need a godly male influence in their lives.

"Daddy, I Need You!"

Every little girl wants to know that her daddy loves her and is proud she is his daughter. She needs a positive, consistent male role model in her life or she will spend her life trying to find one. Girls require male affection from the moment they are born. They crave a father's love; in fact they require it if they are going to mature into healthy young ladies.

Perhaps you are in a situation in which a father's influence is unavailable. If so, ask the Lord to provide someone to stand in the gap. A family member is always the best option.

My mother and father had a rocky marriage. They separated when I was eight, and we moved to Houston to live with my mom's parents. Dad traveled all the time, so even before the separation I didn't see him a lot. In the years to come, especially after Dad's death, I realized what a great gift it was to have my granddaddy in my life as a male role model. He cherished my grandmother, he invested himself in my mother and me, and even though now both of my grandparents are in heaven, I remember the way he remained available if we needed him.

After dinner, he would work for several hours in the library. He had piles of work to do, but if I knocked on the door, he was ready to talk and listen. Even if our time occupied the rest of the evening, he never rushed me away. No deadline was more important than his granddaughter. I'm now in my forties, and I can't recall a time that he did not immediately take my call when I phoned his office.

Still, my father will always be my father. Despite his untimely loss when I was seventeen, I always think about him and look up to him. I always will.

I've come to see that when a father is not a consistent part of a child's life, but instead pops in and out at opportune times, his children begin to idolize him rather than loving and accepting him for who he is in reality. This is where we mothers need to make sure we're communicating with our daughters about their male relationships. What is positive and what is not?

This can mean walking a fine line. Let's be careful in how we share information with our girls because, even though they need a realistic view, their father needs to be respected in their eyes. Focus on doing your best never to criticize your children's father, and if you need to speak critical words for advice or healing, keep your children from hearing you.

A daughter's image of her father often translates into her image of God. If Dad is loving and forgiving, she will view God that way too. If Dad is angry and condemning, those traits will be one of a girl's biggest hurdles in her relationship with God. The way our daughters relate to men and to God must be carefully observed and gently addressed.

An absentee father needs to adjust his priorities and find ways to spend time with his family. If this is simply not possible, he should at least make sure his wife has strong emotional support from friends and family. Otherwise, the kids will be affected, and they may begin to act out in unhealthy ways.

A few years ago, Provident Films released *Courageous*, a film that depicts the importance of a father's role. The theme of the movie is "Honor begins at home." Nathan, one of the protagonists, has a solid marriage and a beautiful teenage daughter. He and his wife talk with their daughter about dating, including what kind of guy they would encourage her to spend time with and how to set healthy boundaries. Nathan takes his daughter to dinner and gives her a promise ring that seals her commitment to stay pure until marriage. He then takes an active role in the life of the young man she is drawn to; the young man clearly does not hold her same values, but it's because he needs guidance and discipleship.

Rather than arbitrarily banning his daughter from talking to this man, Nathan lovingly leads as his daughter's father by allowing him to join their family times and spending one-on-one time with him. Nathan provides protection in a way that builds a healthy relationship rather than a barrier that leads to rebellion. This is a beautiful picture of how a father can love a daughter well.[1]

Being a father is a high calling. If your daughter's father does not know and accept that truth, pray and lovingly remind him how much she needs his love. If he doesn't hear you, pray that God will meet her needs—and yours.

She's Twelve Going on Twenty

How a girl feels about herself and the way she relates to others are greatly influenced by her placement in the family. Is she an only child, or does she have brothers and sisters?

According to *The Birth Order Blues* author Meri Wallace, the oldest child "basks in her parents' undivided love and attention for a period of time and often benefits emotionally and intellectually from this experience. She can emerge with a sense of security and self-confidence. However, she also faces some difficult emotional challenges," including high expectations and pressure to succeed.[2]

Wallace continues, "The secondborn child benefits from calmer, more self-confident parents and enjoys the special attention [she] receives as the baby. . . . A secondborn child often feels jealous [of] . . . [and] rejected by" a dominating older sibling. The middle child gains from being both the older and the younger sibling; however, she also experiences jealousy and rejection. Often she is chasing to catch up to the older sibling and rushing to keep ahead of the younger. Her biggest struggle is establishing her own identity.[3]

The only child has plenty of identity with her parents' full attention, but she often feels lonely. The baby has a special spot in the family and is generally loved by all. She is exposed to a lot more at an early age, and she wants to emulate the others and tends to learn from their mistakes. She also enjoys the most relaxed parents! In a large family where the roles are not so clearly defined, it is vital that all the children feel valued.

These are textbook examples, but they can help us gain a little more insight into how to understand our children according to their placement in the family.

I once saw a story of a fifteen-year-old girl, the middle daughter of three children close in age, who was found murdered in the doorway of her room. When the police started investigating, they made a shocking discovery. The older brother (by fifteen months) had seemed distressed and angry when told about his sister's death, but later, when confronted with the holes in his story, he finally confessed. He had murdered his sister.

Family and friends were dumbfounded when the brother admitted his guilt and his motive. He was jealous of his sister. She was younger but seemed to excel in everything. He could not stand the thought of living a lifetime in competition with a girl—*that* girl, his sister.

Siblings need to have respect reinforced in the home. This will create the bedrock for communication. Our children will learn how to treat one another—or how *not* to treat one another—by watching the adults interact within the home. When Mom and Dad show respect to each other and to each of their children, the children will emulate that behavior. When parents pit one child against another, or favor one child unfairly, or make one of their children a laughingstock, damage is done that will last a lifetime.

I have never seen a "perfect family with perfect children." I remember taking the children to dinner one night when several people commented, "Your children are so well behaved! Ours were never that good in public at that age." A few nights later we were out to dinner again. That night the kids were completely out of control—same kids, similar situation, entirely different response. Kids will be kids, but we are responsible for how they treat one another.

As your little girl becomes a young lady, her hormones will

cause her to change the way she handles conflict. Her once-beloved sister may become her worst enemy. Or her annoying older brother may suddenly be the object of her secret gratitude because he brings home an endless array of good-looking guys from school. The key to having a harmonious home during this time is open, honest, and constant communication between siblings and parents. One wise mom told me that she would rather see her children in the kitchen, having a yelling match, than cooped up in their separate bedrooms with the music blasting and the doors shut.

It's up to us to instill love and respect in our children for one another. We can't do it by encouraging competition between them, or by taking sides in their disputes, or by yelling at them to shut up. Instead, we need to do all we can do, twenty-four hours a day, seven days a week, to create a home environment in which family love and respect can be built into genuine, life-long friendship, loyalty, and camaraderie.

When Friends Seem as Important as Family

In the movie *Wide Awake*, the lead is a fifth-grade boy who spends the year observing and exploring life and interpersonal relationships. At the end he writes: "Before fifth grade there were Ninja Turtles . . . boys were boys for no reason, weirdos were weird, and daredevils were not afraid of anything. . . . Now there are family, friends, and girls. Before this year, the people I loved lived forever. I spent this year looking for something. Like I was asleep before and finally woke up and went, I'm wide awake now."[4]

As kids grow, they will turn to someone for answers. If it isn't their family, then it will be their friends. As we have discussed in earlier chapters, friends play an enormous role in our daughters' lives, and that means peer pressure is a real issue.

Kelly changed schools and met a girl named Kate. Kate seemed to have everything going her way—cool parents, decent grades, a cute boyfriend, and great clothes. Kate gradually began to introduce Kelly to a different way of life. It was a fast life, where grades were achieved dishonestly, where friends were the focus and their opinions mattered more than family, where parties were the norm, and where drugs, sex, and alcohol were allowed by Kate's parents.

All this was eye-opening and invigorating for Kelly, who had lived a pretty normal and, she thought, boring life. She began to discover a side of herself that she did not know existed. She dressed differently, her taste in music changed, and her whole perspective on life started to shift. Her parents saw a difference, but they didn't pick up on anything worrisome at first. Her grades were acceptable, and she had friends and seemed happy. What more could they desire?

They first recognized a problem when they discovered that Kelly was lying about her activities. On Saturdays she often told them that she was sleeping over and going to church with a friend the next morning, but her parents unexpectedly discovered that this was not true. Then one Friday night there came a phone call that Kelly's mom would never forget. A police officer explained that Kelly had been arrested at a downtown club for using drugs and participating in prostitution.

Kelly's parents were devastated. And thus began a long road to recovery for the whole family. By God's grace, their efforts were successful. Today Kelly is a senior in high school. She is teaching dance at a local studio after school. She has been accepted into a great university, and she has a growing and vibrant walk with the Lord.

Could that same phone call ever come to your house or to mine? With God's help, I pray it never does. A proverb says, "A young woman is known by the friends she keeps." Let's make sure we know just exactly which friends our daughters are keeping. We'll be more likely to know by making sure our homes are havens, places of peace and love for everyone who passes through their doors—family and friends alike.

Moms & Daughters: Working It Out Together

1. Have Family Night once a week. For example, every Tuesday night pick a restaurant or an activity out of a hat. Go out together and have fun!

2. Make your house a place of peace and safety for all. Also, do what you can to make it a fun place for your kids to hang out, with or without friends.

3. Practice giving guidance with questions rather than unsolicited answers.

Music and Media

Every time I hear the old song "The Things We Do for Love," I think about my seventh-grade crush, Joe Wolf. Even though many years have passed since I saw him, and time has erased many memories from junior high school, the sound of that song instantly flashes me back to those days, and to the feelings of infatuation I experienced. Music has an amazing stronghold on the mind and the heart. Somehow it can instantly touch our souls and change our moods.

Have you listened to the music kids are hearing these days? Who are their favorite bands? What are the lyrics they're singing? What are our kids feeding into their souls?

Most people don't buy a book and memorize it in its entirety. Yet when my daughter buys a CD or downloads a song, she knows it by heart after listening to it only a few times. In our family, we often listen to Christian music exclusively. Still, the secular influence is present. Older children are much more in tune with guy-girl relationships because of their exposure to songs that emphasize love from the world's point of view.

Songs like these focus on so-called *love*—a well-worn version of the word—which essentially means "finding *total fulfillment* in another person." Of course, that view of love is a dangerous idea, because no one can fulfill the deep longings in our hearts; only the Lord can completely satisfy our deepest needs. However, the picture that is painted through music and media portrays life and love as a fairy tale or as a Greek tragedy. Meanwhile, real life is not usually lived to that extreme.

In the sixties, Woodstock and its songs about freedom influenced an entire generation. Dress, talk, and lifestyles previously unheard-of became acceptable. In the seventies, we saw the emergence of contemporary Christian music. This gave godly parents an outlet for their children, providing a way in which kids could enjoy current musical styles with lyrics that had a positive influence. Still, the exposure to all types of music is unavoidable. As moms, let's be prepared to guide, and yet avoid being in absolute control, when it comes to our daughters' music.

Stephanie is now in her thirties. She listens to secular music most of the time and doesn't really pay attention to the ratings on movies. Stephanie admits she is more focused on the right parts of life when she listens to Christian music and is influenced by wholesome media, but she grew up not being allowed to watch certain movies or listen to the radio, so today she loves the freedom to make her own choices. Now that she's

She's Twelve Going on Twenty

a mom, she agrees with the principles of her upbringing, but she wants to communicate her concerns about media influence in a way that won't lead to rebellion in her children.

Her tactic is to listen with them to a new CD, or to sit with them and watch a TV show together. Afterward, they have a discussion. If her kids' friends are raving about a PG-13 movie, Stephanie will review it and then decide if her children can see it too. She has found that being actively involved and discussing her reasons for rejecting certain kinds of music, shows, or other media options helps her kids make healthy choices individually. Her prayer is that they will continue to do so when they are on their own.

Sometimes bands with foul mouths and terrible subject matter play entertaining music. And it is important for our children to learn to discern. By pointing out what's positive and what's negative, we can help them recognize the difference. Let's teach them to say, "They're an awesome band—it's too bad they use such bad language." Or, "I think they've got a great drummer, but they mostly sing about suicide, and I feel sad when I hear that message."

Good News and Bad News

Teens have innumerable media options. These all link together and provide exposure to lifestyles and attitudes that would never have come across a nine- to twelve-year-old's path even ten years ago. Our kids are often much more informed than we are, and they are interested in keeping up with more than the latest styles.

A survey by *Seventeen* magazine found that 45 percent of teens read, watch, or listen to the news every day. Four percent of teens believe that the media story is always true, compared to 68 percent who think most stories are right on target. Twenty-eight percent of teens are more skeptical and believe that the media get stories wrong just as much as they get them right. Overall, 57 percent said they trusted the media, and 49 percent of teens felt that the newspaper was the most credible source of information.[1] In 2012, a Nielsen survey revealed that 58 percent of all online users think "owned media," such as messages on company websites, is trustworthy, and 50 percent believe information they receive in their e-mail.[2]

This book was first written after the Clinton scandals and the Littleton, Colorado, tragedy. Parents all over the country began to wonder if they should limit their children's access to television news. It is an interesting question, especially now that situations that seemed to belong only in movies are happening consistently. From the midnight movie shooting at the opening of *The Dark Knight Rises* in Aurora, Colorado, to the horrifying school shooting at Sandy Hook Elementary in Connecticut right before Christmas, both in 2012, one can only imagine what it's like for our daughters, who are now in a world where this violence is horrible but not unusual. How can we as moms walk through this kind of exposure to tragedy in a way that builds character, concern, and prayerful grief within the souls of our daughters? If watching the news as a family provides an opportunity for parents and kids to involve themselves in quality conversations, then it can turn into a worthwhile activity. However, if our girls are left on their own to sort out the newsroom's blurred ethics, exaggerated threats, and the tabloid approach to life, they will surely find themselves confused and afraid.

Have you taken the time to talk about the news with your daughter? Have you discussed the media's role in our culture, and the way journalism influences lifestyles? As our girls get older, they will need some guidance in weighing the facts against the hype and finding a solid foundation for what they believe and what they don't believe. As Christian parents, we should try to become the best guides and teachers possible.

Caught in the Web

For many girls in our daughters' generation, an e-mail address has taken the place of a phone number. The Internet allows all kind of purchases—everything from jewelry to prescription drugs to groceries—to be bought at home. Families used to connect with communities; now the world is brought to the family on a little screen.

Neil Postman wrote a powerful book called *Technopoly,* a term used by Postman to describe our turn-of-the-century media culture. Being media-conscious not only means that we align ourselves with "technophiles," but that we also recognize that with the convenience of each new technological development, there are dangers that can threaten our children's future. Postman states, "A new technology does not add or subtract something. It changes everything. . . . When an old technology is assaulted by a new one, institutions are threatened. When institutions are threatened, a culture finds itself in crisis. . . . Educators ask, Will students learn mathematics better by computer than by textbooks?"[3] Our children may choose never to leave home for university. It's becoming common for students to get a college diploma by attending computer classes in their very own rooms. Technology is constantly evolving.

Most parents know to set passwords to block their children from accessing inappropriate parts of the Internet. And the World Wide Web has been a wonderful tool for school projects, games, and access to current information on all sorts of subject matter. Being online can occupy a child for hours, but not without danger.

Besides the obvious trap of readily available pornography, these mediums pose other dangerous aspects. As wonderful as advancing technology is for communicating with friends and relatives, it also opens the door to exposure to people with ulterior motives. This is especially true when it comes to our young daughters. You have probably heard as many stories as I have about kids communicating with strangers. Without warning, unthinkable things can happen. Now, social media and texting are more popular ways of communicating, and actually are more daunting when misused, but thankfully kids are more informed. Although the following story occurred a decade ago, it highlights the pitfalls of the way kids communicate through technology (at that time, through e-mail and "chatting"). It still serves as a cautionary tale for parents today.

Fourteen-year-old Connie spent her afternoons alone. Her mom had to work, and her brother had football practice, so she whiled away the lonely hours chatting on the Internet. One rainy afternoon, Connie's life was brightened up when she met a new guy online. Over a few months, they chatted several times a day. Finally, he asked to meet her. He told her that he was sixteen, had blond hair and blue eyes, and was built like Justin Timberlake.

Connie was overjoyed when they finally set a time and place for a meeting. She sent a text to her mom and brother in case she wasn't back when they arrived home. The message said, "I didn't tell you what I was doing because I knew that you would disapprove, but I've met the most incredible guy over the Internet and he wants to meet me. (He says that he looks like Justin Timberlake.) I'll be home for dinner and maybe he will come with me. I'll be at the McDonald's near the house. Please don't be mad! Love, Connie."

They received her message at 6:30. The manager at the McDonald's remembered seeing Connie at about 4:30. He said that she left with a gentleman who was forty-five or fifty. She went willingly, he said. We can only speculate that this dangerous man claimed to be the boy's father and conned her into letting him take her to his "son." One week later Connie's body was found in the trunk of an abandoned car thirty-five miles out of town.

How could anyone get that convinced? It goes back to influence. Remember when the Internet phenomenon brought the romantic movie *You've Got Mail* to the screen? It promised to turn every computer encounter into a fabulous relationship. Now such expectations are easier to comprehend. The Internet is no longer new, and it has become the norm for many happily married couples to have started their relationships online.

It is imperative that we educate our girls about the technological dangers that face them every day. If you're like me, you'll have to educate yourself first, because our kids know and understand more about technology than many moms. Just as we "go back to school again" with our kids' academic pursuits, we also need to reeducate ourselves about the changing technological times.

Television, Movies, and Video Games

My friend Muriel is a visual learner. She retains everything she sees but has a hard time remembering what she has read, even if she read it just the night before. This is a common story among many kids today because they have grown up with the media providing instant answers and gratification. Muriel's parents have decided to eliminate television on Monday through Thursday and limit but allow it Friday through Sunday.

Several of the books Muriel is reading for school have been made into movies. These films have been helpful tools for her; after she has read the book, the movie helps her better understand the sequence and characters. She has advanced significantly in her academics through educational video games and computer programs. As much as media can be a detriment to our girls' growth and development, when used wisely, they can also be a powerfully effective mechanism for learning.

However, it can be alarming to research the movies that are marketed to teens. One of the older movies that sent up a red flag was *Pleasantville*. The theme of the movie was that growth and freedom are found through breaking out of your "safe box" and realizing that life becomes colorful and exciting when someone openly expresses herself. This open expression was displayed in the movie as the ability to explore physically through sex, oral sex, masturbation, and extramarital affairs.

In the film, these things brought a teenager's (and her family's) world to life. This same kind of theme seems to be repeated again and again in movies geared to reach teenagers. I remember seeing *Grease* in high school with my boyfriend. Yes, that was a very long time ago, but the medium brought passion to the forefront of our thoughts that night, and afterward things started to get out of hand. Thankfully, standards were already set and self-control won the battle.

Considering the explicit—not implied—sex acted out before the eyes of young kids, some of them not yet teenagers, it is a miracle that our girls aren't completely engrossed in an immoral lifestyle. It has all become so dangerously "normal." If my kids really want to see a certain movie or television show, I've learned to preview it first and then decide.

As a family, we sit down together and watch television shows and then discuss the content. There are only a few shows that we all conclude are okay. The reality-TV shows that center around musical talent have become popular in our home. These are generally safe choices. Who would openly welcome a murderer, a witchcraft practitioner, or a display of adultery into our living rooms? Yet we allow it into our lives every time the TV stays on and is not carefully monitored.

Video games have increased in popularity since arriving on the scene in the 1980s. The overall realistic quality and interactive nature of the current video games have magnified the impact of this form of entertainment to a whole new level, especially in the lives of adolescents. Consider this research, summarized by the Palo Alto Medical Foundation, which discusses the link between video games and increased aggressiveness in teenagers:

Part of the increase in aggressive behavior is linked to the amount of time children are allowed to play video games. In one study by Walsh (2000), a majority of teens admitted that their parents do not impose a time limit on the number of hours they are allowed to play video games. The study also showed that most parents are unaware of the content or the Entertainment Software Rating Board (ESRB) rating . . . of the video games their children play.

In another study conducted by Gentile, Lynch, Linder & Walsh (2004, p. 6) . . . the authors also stated that teens who play violent video games for extended periods of time:

- Tend to be more aggressive
- Are more prone to confrontation with their teachers
- May engage in fights with their peers
- See a decline in school achievements. (Gentile et al, 2004).[4]

This is powerful research that we cannot ignore. Video games are not babysitters for our children. Yet some games, like *Guitar Hero* and many of the options for the Wii, can become a really fun family affair. As my children were growing up, we had a rule that someone trusted (sometimes but not always me) would play and approve each new game before it was allowed. The kids would sometimes try to sneak banned games in, but then we would look at the game in question and discuss why it is not allowed in our home.

Media, in its many forms, will overtake our lives and families if we allow it to creep into our homes and influence our lives and, most of all, our children. Let's take the time to pay attention and monitor its entrance before it becomes a mainstay.

Social Media and Smartphone Mania

How true is the saying "The one constant in life is change!" Ten years ago I never knew there would be words like *Facebook*, *Twitter*, *Instagram*, *Tumblr*, and *Keek*, to name a few. Texting is the norm of the day, and teens texting while driving causes more teenage deaths than drunk driving.[5] In the time it takes to send or read a text—4.6 seconds—a driver moving at 55 miles per hour has driven the length of a football field with her eyes off the road.[6]

I remember getting my first "car phone." It was a monstrosity that sat on the console of my car, and I was only allowed to use it for emergencies because it was so expensive. Now it is common to see even small children with their own iPhones, iPods, and iPads. Our girls are in constant communication with the world through these mediums.

It's wonderful to keep in touch with each other, especially with family who may not live close. Remember when Skype was something used to talk with people on other continents? Skyping is still a great way for a soldier to see his new baby, or for grandparents to spend time with their grandchildren if they're unable to travel, or for any of us to talk face-to-face with the people we love. Now we have FaceTime as a way of keeping in touch with even those in our everyday lives.

The new ways of communicating have taken away the need for human interaction in order to feel close to another person. Before these social media options emerged, we got together to talk and catch up. Now, you can just look on people's Facebook pages to feel close to them instantly. You can keep up with their lives, and they with yours, without ever talking on the phone or in person. This is where we have the chance to step in as moms. We can say, "This is fun, but let's invite your friends over after school." If we encourage our girls to have the cute boy they're "talking to" come over for dinner or go to a sporting event with the family, it brings in a "real life" element before the relationship gets established.

As adults we have to get great at texting if we want to communicate with our kids. Texting is easier than a full-fledged phone call, but often it's *too* easy. Has your daughter ever gone crazy over a text from a school crush—and yet they have never even talked to each other? A boy may not have an actual conversation with a girl, but usually he can get her to agree to "hang out," maybe at the mall or the movies. The line between getting together in groups and being able to date is completely blurred. Through social media, the natural progression of learning basic information about each other and getting to know someone is often done before two people ever meet or spend time talking. This sets the stage for relationships that rapidly progress and often become intensely physical upon the first meeting.

My kids document everything. It used to be e-mailing pictures; then it was posting on Facebook; now it's a continual, moment-by-moment account of our life and activities on Instagram or a thirty-second video on Keek. The traditional ways of relating—writing letters, making phone calls, and so on—are foreign to most kids, while smartphones give kids access to social media wherever they go.

My best friend, Mary, has an awesome husband and three boys. Several years ago they started a tradition of taking one or two weeks once a year to go away to a lake house near the mountains. While away, they put up their phones, computers, and other technological devices, and just interact with each other. They read, talk, play board games, go hiking, and do other activities that tend to become a lost art in families who find themselves entrenched in social media. And no, Mary and her family are not on a reality-TV show—they actually want to be together! The kids love the time away and look forward to it every year. I am working to make a similar tradition for our family as well. Even if you can't take a full week, take a few days or a weekend to get away from all our global connectors.

One evening one of my daughter's friends was over for dinner, and she didn't understand why our family turned our phones facedown on the table while we ate.

I told her that if we didn't, we might as well eat by ourselves! It's hard enough to find an evening to sit down together for a meal; we don't need to take away from that precious time by allowing interactions with people not at the table—or allowing the kids to text each other, leaving out the adults.

The biggest challenge of this media age is how to have face-to-face interaction. As parents, let's look for the upside to technology and be proactive so we don't find ourselves taken over by it in a way that leads to little human interaction, especially with those we treasure the most.

Parental Peer Pressure

My friend Dana has two children: one is twelve and the other is fourteen. She says that her biggest battle right now is the peer pressure she feels from her friends. I looked at her questioningly and said, "Your daughter's peer pressure?" And she said, "No, Kim. My peer pressure to let my daughter do what her friends are doing."

She and her husband, John, have an incredible relationship built on love, trust, and respect. This has always been evident to me. And the traits that have blessed their marriage have filtered into their relationship with their children. Because there is trust, their daughter does not become depressed or manipulative when told no.

Instead, it's their daughter's friend's *mother* who is upset. One day she wanted to drop off the girls at the mall for a movie. She didn't want her daughter to go alone, and she became upset because none of her daughter's friends were allowed to accompany her. Dana laughed a little—"I feel like I've done something wrong when I say no. But I'm saying it anyway!"

I have great respect for John and Dana for not sheltering their children. They simply protect them from being exposed to certain experiences too soon. Dana recently shared a great insight with me: "We want our daughter to know that each of her experiences is a privilege, not a right. Helping her understand that is just one more step toward growth and maturity. It's our hope that we are enabling our daughter to make wise choices when we are no longer there to give guidance."

She's Twelve Going on Twenty

Praying for Discernment

As mothers, we can guard our children from the dangers of the media. But our role needs to focus on something much deeper—what are the aims of our daughters' hearts? Is it their intent to seek purity and to have integrity when using these media? Are they consumed with curiosity, or driven by rebellion?

As they voice their questions and want to see certain shows or listen to questionable music, it's our job to make sure that we join them in their quest. It's up to us to teach our girls how to be discerning, and why a Christian woman must limit the things she allows into her soul. Then God's Spirit within our daughters will answer their questions about whether a lyric or a story line or a social media outlet will glorify God and move them forward in life.

Of course this doesn't mean everything acceptable is solely Christian. God wants us to enjoy many aspects of life and music, literature, movies, and television that speak about life in diverse ways. As our daughters grow, they will develop a moral grid through which to sift information and either allow or not allow it into their lives.

Our parenting paths must be illuminated by godly wisdom. Only God can help us know, understand, and interpret each new technological opportunity that appears on our daughters' horizons. Meanwhile, let's teach them to pray, and pray with them the ancient prayer of the Hebrew king David: "Search me, God, and know my heart; test me and know my anxious thoughts. See if there is any offensive way in me, and lead me in the way everlasting" (Ps. 139:23–24 NIV).

Moms & Daughters:
Working It Out Together

1. With your daughter, listen to some of her favorite songs. Talk about the music and evaluate the lyrics together.

2. Watch her favorite TV show together and discuss it with her. Try to find something positive to say along with your criticism.

3. Take her to a movie that you know promotes wholesome values, and talk about why it's worth seeing.

4. In your mother-daughter journal, write how TV, books, movies, and so on have affected each of you, for better or for worse.

5. Discuss the dangers of the Internet. Regularly check out what websites she's been visiting and with whom she is communicating.

Boys and Falling in Love

Ever since Kaitlin was a little girl, she has dreamed about finding her one true love. She's watched *The Sound of Music* over and over again with her parents. She and her friends cried every time they saw *Ever After* (the Cinderella love story with Drew Barrymore), and they saw it six times in a row. And lately, they discovered the Twilight series, reading each book and eagerly awaiting the movie openings.

With soft images and soaring music, Hollywood beautifully portrays the dream of everlasting love. And girls—like Kaitlin, like your daughter, and like mine—long for that dream to become their reality. The question is, can it? What happens after the kiss? Does the marriage really last forever? Is there a "match made in heaven" for each of us?

These are questions that too many women ask themselves

only after they are faced with a broken relationship or a struggling marriage. "How did I get here?" they wonder. "All I ever wanted was the dream."

Most movies don't show the struggle. The ones that do show the struggle get great reviews, but nobody wants to see them. So how can we help our daughters leave the fantasy behind? How can we guide them into making healthy choices when dealing with opposite-sex relationships? How can we prepare them to walk into marriage with their eyes wide open to the challenges, the struggles, the joys, and the triumphs?

Joanna, newly single, knew too well that after a failed marriage, women often feel beaten down and unable to stand strong. Like many divorced women, she felt insecure and hurt. Joanna attracted a man who wanted to rescue her family and to show her how to really be loved. He appeared so noble, but eventually she saw that their relationship was more about him building his self-esteem than about recognizing and receiving God's gift humbly, with a desire to honor God together. She sought the Lord, and she realized that like her, this man was also "in process." Together they discovered that they both had the desire to shift their focus from each other to the Lord. In time, Joanna knew that this man became the "right one" for her.

I asked them, "How do all of these feelings work together with what we are called to be in God's Word?" How can we as moms coming out of a failed marriage teach our daughters how to love well in a healthy way that builds a solid foundation? They pointed me to 1 Corinthians 13:4–8:

This love of which I speak is slow to lose patience—it looks for a way of being constructive. It is not possessive: it is

She's Twelve Going on Twenty

neither anxious to impress nor does it cherish inflated ideas of its own importance.

Love has good manners and does not pursue selfish advantage. It is not touchy. It does not keep account of evil or gloat over the wickedness of other people. On the contrary, it is glad with all good men when truth prevails.

Love knows no limit to its endurance, no end to its trust, no fading of its hope; it can outlast anything. It is, in fact, the one thing that still stands when all else has fallen. (PHILLIPS)

As I read these truthful words, I felt a deep conviction that led to the question, is this how we love?

Responding to the "Right One"

Beth's hometown finally had a hockey team, and one of the players had a handsome son named Adam, who went to her school. He had brown hair and blue eyes and an inviting boyish smile. He seemed to notice Beth right away, and all the girls were soon saying, "Isn't he cute?" and "He likes you, Beth." Within forty-eight hours, Beth was lost in a daydream. She thought about Adam all day and dreamed about him all night. She knew almost nothing about him, except that he was really cute, his father was a famous hockey player, and he was paying attention to her. What more was there to know? Beth was in love!

First impressions are usually based on outward appearances. Even though the spiritual approach would be to look at the heart over the head, when it comes to romance, physical attraction definitely plays a powerful part in a budding relationship. When romance is in the air during the adolescent years, soul nearly always eclipses spirit. And for girls as young as our daughters, the chance of making love last a lifetime is remote anyway. So their intense crushes are chuckled about and encouraged, no matter what the young man is really like on the inside.

A few years ago I read about teenage boys describing the most romantic thing they have ever done for their girlfriends. One guy, Mark, wrote a poem for his girlfriend and gave her seven roses on Valentine's Day for their seven months of "going out." Eric took his girlfriend to her favorite restaurant and hired a musician to serenade her. Of course, she loved it.

For whatever reason, girls crave romance. And if we moms don't talk to our daughters about this, we can expect them to be influenced by a media that says, "Romance is everything!" Instead of feeding the fires of infatuation, let's take a different approach. Let's sit down with our daughters, as young as they are, and help them make a list of the qualities they want in a guy. My twelve-year-old cousin and I made a list, and hers was about as direct as it could be. It went like this: (1) great eyes; (2) good family; (3) romantic; (4) outgoing; (5) leader. Those were the top five criteria.

One of the primary sources of fascination between boys and girls is that the sexes really don't understand each other, and the less they understand, the more intrigued they are. A teen magazine talked about the ultimate "guy mysteries." Here are a few:

1. How can they get ready in under two minutes and still look so incredibly cute?
2. Why don't they need to carry a purse? Where's all their "stuff"?
3. How can they remember all those baseball signals and then forget something like your birthday?

Guys wonder about us too. Here are a few girl mysteries:

1. Why do girls have to go to the bathroom in groups?
2. Why the shoe obsession?
3. Why do they like to go to movies that cause them to weep uncontrollably?

So is there really "one"? Some people adamantly say yes. Others aren't so sure. If you talk to people with successful marriages, they often talk about their first meeting. The guy usually says, "I knew the moment I saw her that she was the one." Now, how can someone know that without even having one conversation? It's unexplainable.

Yet there is a certain God-given chemistry that sparks and ignites—sometimes at first glance—and the warm glow it creates is impossible to ignore. In Genesis 29 we read the story of Jacob and Rachel. Jacob went to live with and work for his uncle Laban. When he first arrived, he met Laban's daughter Rachel. There was an instant connection.

Laban hired Jacob, and because of his love for Rachel (notice he had just arrived, so it was an immediate response), Jacob offered to work for seven years to earn her hand in marriage. Those seven years seemed only a few short days because of his love for her. Then the day of reckoning came, and Laban tricked Jacob by giving him his older daughter, Leah.

Laban explained this treachery by saying that it was not customary for the younger daughter to marry before the older. Jacob did receive Rachel as his wife after another week, but he still had to work seven more years. Leah was a lovely girl, but she wasn't "the one." Jacob loved Rachel.

I remember a time when I picked up my kids at camp, and fifteen-year-old Maxfield, my eldest son, ran up to introduce me to the most beautiful girl. He couldn't wait to share how they met. A few nights before, the group was having an intense prayer time, and everyone joined hands. After the prayer, my son looked up into the beautiful blue eyes of the girl he'd been holding hands with, and he felt an instant connection. He was sure he'd met the girl he might marry.

For a few years they visited each other during the school year breaks, and they thought God had called them to marriage one day. But after they didn't go to camp together for a couple years, they drifted apart. Now, they are just friends, but they have an incredible bond. This is how God designed relationships to begin: by attending church together, holding hands, praying together. We do these things when in a healthy, growing relationship.

Maxfield had a taste of true intimacy, but as he matured and started to date, he learned that sometimes we do these things to *feel* close without *getting* close. We keep what appears to be a healthy boundary, but we feed our need for intimacy in a counterfeit way. At a relatively young age, Maxfield was able to recognize that there was a difference, but he later asked questions about what exactly the difference was. He began to understand that a healthy relationship progression involves taking steps forward, with the support of family, friends, mentors, and church family, while moving from friends to courting to engagement to marriage. A person in an unhealthy relationship is afraid of these steps.

Keeping a relationship at the "just church" or "just walks" stage can be okay as long as it's not a setup for one day letting down the guard so things get out of hand and go to an engagement or marriage level without the healthy steps. When that happens, often the couple finds themselves in a scary situation as they have to deal with the physical intimacy issue before it's time. They may battle, draw close, and pull apart, all laying the groundwork for a fear of intimacy. As mothers, let's pray that God will build true intimacy in our daughters' relationships rather than needing to create a protective barrier that keeps others from getting too close.

What a gift it is to pass on to a daughter the foresight and the wisdom to wait for the "right" one—the one God has chosen for her, the one whom she will truly love and the one who will treasure her after he says, "I do!" Let's pray that she will wait for a man with whom she can walk through any and all of the joys and sorrows of life, to have and to hold. But what shall we tell her about that "spark"? Will it be an important factor in her decision of whom to marry? Yes! Will it be the primary factor? No!

Making Love . . . Last: Physical Relationship

Morri came in from her first school dance, which she had attended with her first official high school boyfriend, and walked right upstairs to go to sleep. Her brother, who picked her up, told her parents, "Let her be. It was not a good night." She had called to get picked up thirty minutes early. Something was up.

The next day, Morri shared about the dance. She went on to explain that during the dance, she went to the restroom and came back to find a girl dancing with her boyfriend in a way that was more than friendly. Morri waited for a few minutes and decided to leave.

At school the next day, Morri found out that when the girl heard Morri had gone home, she was very concerned that Morri was mad at her for dancing with her boyfriend. He himself felt terrible and had tried to reach her when he realized she had left.

At school Morri's friends told her, "It's a party. That's what people do at parties—they dance. It's not like he would hang out with any other girl if it wasn't the school dance." They asked if she felt jealous.

Morri said, "No, I know he likes me. It just felt disrespectful to me that he would let a girl come up and dance with him like that when *I* don't even dance that way. I also was surprised my friend thought it was okay to seek him out when I was gone." She went on to explain that people told her she should have gone on the dance floor and let her boyfriend know she was back. Morri replied that that's what would have happened if he had not been dancing so intimately with her friend.

Among her peers, Morri gained a lot of respect that day. Her friends came back and told her that she set the standard and raised the bar when it comes to relationships and what is appropriate and respectful. Both she and her boyfriend are committed to abstinence, a decision that shapes the boundaries in their relationship. Morri wasn't trying to be cool or right or to make a scene—she just wanted to honor God and give space for her boyfriend to lead and make decisions about who he wants to be, both in a relationship and before God.

What builds a relationship so that it will endure? We have already noted the importance of physical attraction, but let's take this subject a little further. Moms, we know that when two people start taking steps in the physical area, it clouds the formation of the relationship and often allows unhealthy emotional patterns to evolve. Too often an innocent kiss can quickly escalate a relationship to sexual intercourse, which is designed for marriage. What physical expressions of affection are allowed in a dating relationship, and where is the line drawn?

It's important for our daughters to recognize that the progression between a boy and a girl, or a man and a woman, is much more than "Did you get to first, second, or third base?" As a boy initiates interest, a girl can choose to respond or retreat. With each step she allows, she is inviting him to further explore her world. And when a girl (or a woman) sets appropriate standards physically, it gives her the freedom to see beyond his boyish charm and into his heart. As parents, we have an obligation to provide godly guidance for our children within our homes. Deuteronomy 6:5–7 gives wise counsel to parents:

"You shall love the LORD your God with all your heart and with all your soul and with all your might. These words, which I am commanding you today, shall be on your heart. You shall teach them diligently to your [daughters] and shall talk of them when you sit in your house and when you walk by the way and when you lie down and when you rise up."

Christy and Bob started hanging out together in ninth grade. Since they weren't old enough to date, they spent a lot of time at each other's houses. This seemed like a great idea because their parents were home, but as they looked back years later after they were married and had children, they decided some things weren't as healthy as they'd seemed. Christy and Bob had struggled with sexuality all through high school and college. It became a constant battle.

It started when Christy's parents went to sleep and allowed Bob to stay at the house with her, watching movies. They now realize that their parents should have been more involved, either by staying up until Bob left or by asking him to leave when they went to bed. Instead, the parents chose the "kids-will-be-kids" approach.

It's important that we give our children freedom in a controlled environment. However, we must not create compromising situations in the name of trust. Put yourself in your daughter's shoes. Allow her to make her own choices, but don't be naive enough to set her up for a fall.

"Guard Your Heart": Emotional Relationship

Proverbs 4:23 has an important message for all of us. The writer says, "Above all else, guard your heart, for everything you do flows from it" (NIV). In a world where emotions are often allowed to run wild, where they are assumed to be uncontrollable, it is encouraging to know that we are not at the mercy of our "hearts" or our feelings. Our daughters can protect themselves from hurtful or destructive relationships. And they will learn at home, from us, and from their fathers. For it is in the dynamics of the home and family that the young girl's heart and soul are formed and shaped.

In my years of counseling girls, I have noticed that as they begin to form emotional relationships with boys, most times they either remain detached or they latch on for dear life. When a girl remains emotionally detached in a relationship, it is usually because she has not been able to freely express her emotions in her home. Her closed-up and withdrawn emotions demonstrate the way she has learned to relate to others within her family.

But just because a girl is emotionally detached, it doesn't mean that she doesn't get into trouble. A detached girl may be a perfectionist, and her perfectionism will take her sense of order and control to an extreme. Her feelings of self-worth and fulfillment are dependent on having "all her ducks in a row." So even though she seems to have her emotions in check, she will do anything to create the dream of a perfect relationship. This may mean that she allows sexual expression to progress to an unhealthy place in the relationship because she is trying to make everything "perfect." Of course it's done in the name of love, and that seems to justify it.

Then there's the other extreme of the girl who is emotionally dependent. She freely expresses her feelings, and in the process she uses them to her advantage. She may become manipulative and controlling, using tears and smiles to get her way. Deep inside she is so insecure that she wants to validate herself through another person. She knows and puts to use the right words and actions necessary to keep a guy where she wants him—hooked on her.

The guy she attracts may appear to be outgoing, successful, and secure, but deep inside he will most likely be just as lacking in confidence as she is. These two will feed off each other's need for acceptance and unconditional love. But sadly, no matter how deeply they crave fulfillment in one another, their emptiness inside is not—cannot be—filled by any other person.

Our girls don't have to resort to either of these extremes. And now is the time to make sure they don't. When two people form a healthy emotional relationship, it is because two key areas are being met in their lives:

1. They are both content within and thankful for their circumstances.
2. They both receive their worth and acceptance from their personal relationship with Jesus Christ.

Healthy, godly girls attract healthy, godly guys. As we teach our daughters to know and love the Lord, we are not just helping them behave themselves. We are also preparing them to know and love the men the Lord has chosen for them.

A Heart for God: Spiritual Relationship

But the question still remains: When a girl waits for the "right one," how can she know if he has found her? First of all she listens—to hear what he says and how he says it. What is his vision? On what are his eyes focused? Answering those questions will help your daughter determine whether her current heartthrob is the kind of guy who can lead the relationship in the right direction.

In 2 Corinthians 5:17, Paul wrote, "In Christ we are a new creation. Old things are passed away. Behold, new things shall come" (paraphrase). This is the most important quality a girl can look for in a guy. Does he know Jesus as his personal Savior?

I had a friend who always had the same response for any young man who asked her out. She didn't say yes and she didn't say no. She simply said, "Tell me about your relationship with God." Her purpose was to find out if he was a Christian and to see where his focus was in life. This way she didn't find herself spending an evening alone with someone who wasn't seeking God first.

Prayer is another key issue to talk through with our daughters. Prayer builds an incredible bond between two people because together they are entering into spiritual oneness before the Lord.

Ben and Ashley were struggling with their physical relationship when they attended a Young Life camp. There they heard a speaker who motivated both of them to make changes. They knew that the way things had been going was wrong, but somehow it seemed justified. Ben, who lived just down the street, was at Ashley's house, watching a movie. Ashley's parents went to bed (this seems to be a common mistake!), and they decided to pray together so they would be strong and not let things go too far.

Thirty minutes later, their sexual desire was stronger than ever. They stopped before their desires took control, Ben left, and the next day they went to their Young Life leader and asked, "What happened?"

"I'll tell you exactly what happened. You prayed together in a compromising situation," he told them. "Prayer can really bind us together with people of the opposite sex."

But on the other hand, our girls need to look for boys who believe in prayer, who love the Lord, and who sincerely share their desires for chastity and abstinence. Until they meet such boys, as we talk and listen and pray with them, our most important contribution may be in simply telling them that their spiritual life is the place where God's will is first discovered. As He transforms us from within, we are able to know His will (Rom. 12:1–2). That means that girls don't have to "fall" in love with just anybody. God has warned us to guard our hearts, and He will help us to do so—if we'll just ask Him.

What Does God Say to Look for in a Guy?

There are many places in the Bible to look for "great guy qualities." But my favorite resource is Psalm 15. It begins by saying, "O LORD, who may abide in Your tent? Who may dwell on Your holy hill?" The answer is "He who . . .

1. *"walks with integrity, and works righteousness"*—He does what is right when no one is looking.
2. *"and speaks truth in his heart"*—He is honest in thought, word, and deed.
3. *"does not slander with his tongue"*—He does not use his words to hurt others, but speaks the truth in love.

4. *"nor does evil to his neighbor"*—He doesn't hurt others.
5. *"nor takes up a reproach against his friend"*—He does not dump unnecessary rebuke on family or friends.
6. *"in whose eyes a reprobate is despised, but who honors those who fear the LORD"*—He does not look up to those who don't honor the Lord with their lives, but has great respect for those who walk closely with Him.
7. *"swears to his own hurt, and does not change"*—He holds himself accountable even when it's to his disadvantage; even if he could get out of it.
8. *"does not put out his money at interest"*—He is not greedy.
9. *"nor does he take a bribe against the innocent"*—Character is more important to him than money.
10. *"He who does these things will never be shaken."*—He is stable.

Now, who wouldn't want to date and marry a guy like that? Let's make sure our daughters know what to look for and refuse to settle for anything less.

Being the Right Girl for the Right Boy

Psalm 15 doesn't just describe males. It provides good character goals for us, too, both for moms and daughters. And the right kind of young man will be looking at your daughter's character qualities just as she is looking at his. The key word here is *respect*—will he find reason to respect her?

Brigitte is fifteen, and she has decided with her friends that they really don't like the boys in their class. "The older guys are a lot nicer because they treat us with respect, while the boys our own age treat us like buddies. My dad always said that a guy should treat a girl like a delicate flower. Well, according to these guys, we're more like a hedge to be plowed through!"

Brigitte and I talked for a long time about her situation. I told her what a wise woman had once told me: *"You teach people how you want to be treated."*

"You could respond in such a way," I told her, "that will require the guys to change their behavior toward you. And if that doesn't work, they'll at least leave you alone."

Learning to demand respect begins at home. When our daughters feel that we respect them enough to hear and discuss their concerns, they will eventually demand that kind of respect from others. And as our girls mature, they will attract guys who match or exceed their level of maturity, who see them as daughters of the King.

In today's world, girls are often the aggressors in boy-girl relationships. When a girl develops a crush on a boy, unless she is advised otherwise, she may start calling him on the phone continuously, following him around campus, and repeatedly asking him to go out with her. Although there is certainly more freedom for girls to participate in the "dance" than there used to be, that freedom isn't always productive. Nice boys are often driven off by such behavior, avoiding their pursuers at all costs. Other boys are inclined to treat the girls who chase them with disrespect, using them for their self-gratification because they have made themselves too available.

Waiting on the Lord, seeking His will, and trusting in His timing is the most important lesson they can learn about boys and dating. No matter how emotionally captivated they become, if they are committed to God and He is their first love, they will be less likely to find themselves in a disrespectful and heartbreaking relationship.

Learning to Love—God's Way

Falling in love is a misunderstood phrase. Although the emotional feelings may be intense and almost overpowering, when two people start to get to know each other, they aren't really falling; they are *growing* in love. They are taking steps toward each other daily, steps that may sometimes move backward for a while. "The course of true love never did run smooth," Shakespeare wrote.[1] However, if love is allowed to grow slowly, steadily, and wisely, its growth will solidify into the kind of love that will last.

There are many faces of love. Let's focus on three that can be found in the Greek language. *Agape* love is unconditional—the kind of love God has for us. *Phileo* love builds family-type closeness. *Eros* is romantic, passionate love. Couples will often rush to the *eros* stage and then, a few months into the relationship, wonder what went wrong. In reality, both *agape* and *phileo* are far more long-lasting than *eros*. Without a firm foundation of *agape* love, the other loves will eventually erode and collapse.

Our daughters need to understand that when they guard their hearts, if love does not deepen into something lasting, the result is not heartbreak. They have not wounded themselves or compromised their integrity. Instead they have gained a friend.

This is where the groundwork we have laid with our daughters will be tested. If we have invested time and energy in building trust between them and us, they will be more willing to listen when we feel that their boy-girl relationships are progressing too rapidly. When the girls I disciple tell me that they think they have found "the one," I always ask them how their parents feel about the relationship growing toward marriage. If their parents aren't too excited about it, then I encourage them to slow way down.

If marriage is really right today, then it will be right six weeks, six months, or six years from now. God can channel the hearts of kings, turning them wherever He wishes (Prov. 21:1). In the same way, He can channel a couple's hearts to feel at peace with waiting a season before moving into marriage. Time is always on the side of true love.

Now, at the age of nine, twelve, or even sixteen, our daughters are not thinking about marriage, at least not in the immediate future. However, it is during these young years that the process begins. And this is where our role as a trustworthy adviser, who only wants the best for them, is established. Let's be actively involved and always ready to listen. Let's make every effort to offer advice when appropriate and to teach them how to make healthy relational choices on their own. Let's help them recognize the kind of love that will last forever.

Worth the Wait

Because I'm a fourth-generation Texan on both sides of my family, I have a lot of family and friends in Houston, where I spent most of my growing-up years. Jeanette Clift George has been a longtime family friend and a wonderful role model for me. Jeanette is an author and an actress who founded Grace Theatre and Acting School and developed the traveling drama troupe the After Dinner Players. She also starred in the movie *The Hiding Place*, in which she played the role of Corrie ten Boom.

Jeanette Clift became Jeanette Clift George at the age of forty when she married her one true love, Lorraine George. I remember decorating the horse-drawn carriage that romantically whisked them away to their honeymoon. As my mom, sister, grandmother, and I carefully placed flowers and bows on the carriage, our conversation turned to relationships.

At the time, I had dreams of being in love and having a fairy-tale romance. "I hope you will always remember," my grandmother reminded me, "that Jeanette waited on the Lord, and it was worth the wait. Look at all God accomplished through her! And now, after doing so many other worthwhile things, she also gets to enjoy marriage." Forty seemed like old age to me at the time, and I could hardly imagine waiting that long for my own love to come along.

But as I grew into a young woman, Jeanette reminded me that patience was a quality worth praying for. "Rewards," she often said, "follow a lot of prayer and work. And the dream does not come easy." I remembered Jeanette's example when I thought I would marry my high school sweetheart at eighteen and my college beau at twenty. My grandmother and my mom were always quick to remind me about Jeanette, and I'm so glad they did.

I had the privilege of spending some time with Lorraine

and Jeanette a few years ago. It didn't take me long to see that the sweet love they shared at the beginning of their romance was stronger and deeper than ever. I hope I can convey this essential truth to my own daughters: "It is worth the wait." I pray that they will hear the message of patience and faith, loud and clear, at a time when they need it the most.

Brain Chemicals and the Bonding Experience

As we were reminded earlier in the book, God says sin is sin, but sexual sin is against the body and joins two bodies together as one. God designed this union to be shared only between one man and one woman, for pleasure and procreation in marriage. Many Christians are deceived in this arena. Sex with many partners has become common, and it churns my stomach when that fact is coupled with the thought that our bodies are the temples of the Holy Spirit. This is why sex outside of marriage is so dishonoring to the almighty God who created us. However, sex within marriage is not dirty, bad, or hush-hush to God! He created it to be beautiful and to mirror the union Christ has with His bride, the church.

To understand this idea more clearly, it's helpful to study the brain in relation to the way God bonds a man and a woman. Recently, I came across a fascinating book by two doctors, Joe S. McIlhaney Jr. and Freda McKissic Bush, called *Hooked: New Science on How Casual Sex Is Affecting Our Children*. It highlights brain connections and how they affect a man and a woman's ability to have a great, thriving

She's Twelve Going on Twenty

monogamous marriage. The authors state that "short-term, damaging, and often regretted relationships undermine the purpose of bonding hormones such as oxytocin and vasopressin and the purpose of the brain compounding the excitement of sex by producing dopamine."[2]

These chemicals in the brain are defined as follows:

- *Oxytocin*: A neurochemical vital to healthy sex, oxytocin facilitates bonding and builds trust with another person. Both men and women have oxytocin, but it is more active in females. Oxytocin is released by intimate touching with another individual, intercourse, labor and delivery, and nursing.[3]
- *Vasopressin*: Nicknamed "the monogamy molecule," this neurochemical is responsible for two key functions related to relationships: allowing a man to bond to his mate and enabling him to become attached to his children. Vasopressin is "the primary cause of men attaching to women with whom they have close and intimate contact."[4]
- *Dopamine*: A critical messenger chemical, dopamine helps guide human behavior, including motivation and reward. It is the key chemical that promotes risk taking in humans, but it is "values-neutral," so it's easy to get hooked on risky behaviors like sex.[5]

These chemicals have other functions, but you can see how God created them to play a role in sex. McIlhaney and Bush further explain the detrimental effects of serial sex partners:

Men may question why they keep going back to a woman who treats them poorly or may wonder why they never seem able to feel, deep inside, a commitment to a woman after having sex partner after sex partner. Sadly, they simply do not know that their brains are flooded with vasopressin during sexual intercourse and that this neurochemical produces a partial bond with every woman they have sex with. . . . This pattern of having sex with one woman and then breaking up and then having sex with another woman limits them to experience . . . the dopamine rush of sex. They risk damaging a vital, innate ability to develop the long-term emotional attachment that results from sex with the same person over and over. . . .

Their inability to bond after multiple liaisons is almost like tape that loses its stickiness after being applied and removed multiple times.[6]

A Final Word About Love

As moms, our hearts' desire is to see our girls marry the one God has designed for them, the first time. We want our daughters and their mates to trust and grow in love so that it deepens and blossoms over a lifetime. A mother shared this story with her soon-to-be son-in-law the day before the wedding:

Since my daughter was born I have prayed for her husband and asked the Lord to bring her someone like our friend Matthew.

Matthew said the greatest lesson of love he learned

from his father was watching him bring a flower to his mother every day. He didn't understand it until he promised his parents on his wedding day that he would continue the tradition. Once he was married, he had days where he was angry with his wife and wanted to deny her the gift of a flower. It was then that he realized that this one act of love his dad showed to his mom taught him all he needed to know about love, forgiveness, and grace—especially when kids came along and life seemed harder and full of even more relationship challenges.

To give this gift, he had to deal daily with all the "junk" in his own soul and mind that affected his relationship. He learned how to obey God's Word and "be angry, and yet do not sin; do not let the sun go down on your anger" (Eph. 4:26).

The daughter of the mother who told this story continues to thank her mom for sharing it with her husband, because living it out every day has been used by God to save their marriage on more than one occasion!

Moms & Daughters:
Working It Out Together

1. On separate sheets of paper, make lists:
   - your list—qualities you want to see in the guy she marries
   - her list—qualities she wants in the guy she marries

   Compare the lists and discuss them.

2. Write down qualities God wants a woman to look for in a man. Besides Psalm 15, read Titus 1:6–9; 2:6–8; and Galatians 5:16–26.

3. Pray with your daughter that God would bless and protect the man she will one day marry. Pray that He will protect and prepare them for one another.

Competition and Complications with Friends

If your daughters are like mine, friendship means everything to them. Just about every girl wants to find a "best friend," and a beautiful day can be ruined when a friendship is marred by a quarrel or a misunderstanding. Girls seem to be far more committed to their circle of friends than boys. Since it's so important to them, our girls' friendships are something we need to understand and respect.

What makes a friendship last? How can two people build the kind of connections that will last a lifetime? Years ago, Michael W. Smith and his wife, Debbie, wrote an incredible song called "Friends." The chorus tells us that our friends are friends forever if the Lord is the Lord of them. For Christians, the Lord takes friendship to a deeper level and helps it grow.

Tough times and tragedy can also keep friends close. When I was seventeen and my father was killed in a plane crash, three dear friends stuck with me from the moment I heard the news until the burial, which took place in a different city. Those friends are still close to me. These days we live in different states and all of us are busy with our families, yet we have maintained a closeness that picks up whenever we talk or get together.

As our girls begin the journey from grade school into junior high and high school, we can begin to teach them some principles about friendship. And the place to start is by our being a good friend to them. Of course there's more to mothering than being a friend. But even within the parenting role, a friendship can begin to form between our daughters and us when they approach adolescence. And as we model friendship to them, our daughters will have a firsthand example of real friendship.

Friendships Change and Grow

Grace and Karen met the first day of ninth grade. Grace's best friend, Carri, and Karen hit it off too, and the three of them began doing everything together. This was great for Karen because she had instant friends and a chance to get "the lay of the land" at her new school without feeling alone. But by

Christmas break, Karen had figured out that Grace and Carri weren't very "high up" on the social ladder.

Over Christmas, Karen started to make some new friends. She started to dress like the popular girls and hang out with their group. She began by befriending the sister of one of the most popular girls in her class and slowly started getting invited to key parties. After Christmas, Grace and Carri saw the change in her. They felt used and discarded as she moved on to new friendships without including them. The girls all continued to greet one another in the halls, but Grace and Carri got the distinct impression that Karen somehow felt that she was "better" than they were since she had broken into the popular group.

Grace and Carri were great girls who were focused on school and a few close friendships. They continued to like Karen, but they lost a lot of respect for her as they saw how she handled friendships. Besides that, they felt hurt.

It is important for our daughters to understand that people are too important to be used as rungs on a social ladder. As we grow and life carries us forward, we must make sure that we don't leave a lot of wounded people in our paths. Our friendships will change, but each one has played a vital role in shaping who we have become. Every person who crosses our paths, whether tough or terrific, is a unique and valuable blessing. Let's help our girls learn to treasure each person along the way as a gift from God.

When I was in high school, I was given an acronym for "FRIENDS." You may find it helpful to share this with your daughter.

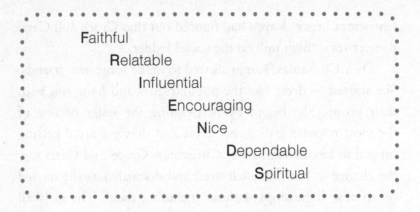

Faithful
Relatable
Influential
Encouraging
Nice
Dependable
Spiritual

Faithful

I once read about a woman in her mideighties who still kept in touch with her high school and college friends from the 1930s. The kind of faithfulness that keeps friends around for decades naturally flows from a heart's desire to stay close but also takes forethought and time. Sending Christmas cards or gifts, or taking time to talk on the phone or get together at least once a year will all build on the camaraderie started early in life to create a treasured lifelong friendship.

The kind of faithfulness that keeps friends around for decades doesn't happen by chance. It involves putting others' interests above our own. Philippians 2:3–4 says, "Let nothing be done through selfish ambition or conceit, but in lowliness of mind let each esteem others better than [herself]. Let each of you look out not only for [your] own interests, but also for the interests of others" (NKJV).

Faithful friends do not make room for selfish ambition.

Nancy and Mindy had been friends since third grade. Their sophomore year of high school was filled with lots of distractions, especially in the area of boys. Mindy was wooed by handsome Tim Johnson, and she knew that he was "the one" for her. They did their best to get the relationship grounded in the right kind of love.

When summer rolled around, Mindy left town for six weeks with her family. Tim called often, and they talked about how much they wished they could be together. Nancy talked to Tim a lot too. Mindy wanted them to be friends because they both were important to her.

After three or four weeks, Nancy arrived to spend some vacation time with Mindy. They were excited to see each other. They talked for hours about Tim, and Mindy couldn't seem to hear enough about him because she missed him so much. But as they talked, Mindy could see a troublesome message written on Nancy's face. Something was wrong. After hours of talking, Nancy broke down and said that she and Tim had gotten too close. They'd been holding hands. And making out. It wasn't love or anything; they were both just lonely.

Mindy was furious and hurt, but mostly she could not believe that Tim had lied to her and said all the things he'd said while he was romancing Nancy. She could have blamed Nancy and ended their friendship, but she had known her for half of her life and she had known Tim for only a year. She was reminded of the proverb that says, "Faithful are the wounds of a friend, but deceitful are the kisses of an enemy" (Prov. 27:6).

It was hard for Nancy to tell the truth because she knew that it would hurt Mindy. But both girls knew that if they cared at all for Tim, he needed to be confronted. They got together, told Tim about their conversation, and ended their respective romances with him. Meanwhile, Mindy and Nancy's friendship grew stronger because of the conflict. It continues to grow ten years later. They still laugh every once in a while about "the Tim encounter," their shared romance.

They ran into Tim recently—he's now happily married with two kids. He told them that their confrontation with him was a turning point in his life because he saw them rise above petty jealousies and anger. They showed true love instead of selfish love to him and to each other. Friendship isn't friendship without faithfulness.

Relatable

Have you spent much time with someone who seems completely focused on superficialities? People like that limit their life experience and their ability to relate to others. When Deanna met Sherry, she thought that she was a sweet girl and started to spend time with her. But the more they were together, the more Deanna began to wonder what was beneath the surface talk. Everything in Sherry's life seemed so perfect.

Deanna felt that she couldn't really open up to Sherry because, being so perfect, she probably wouldn't understand anything that resembled a problem. One time Deanna shared a frustration with her and Sherry answered impatiently. Her tone implied, "I can't believe that you are dealing with that, but since you are, here's how you should handle it." Their friendship did not grow. Deanna couldn't relate to Sherry. Relatable people are real. Sherry wasn't real.

After my father's death, some of my friends approached me and said, "I understand how you feel. I lost my mother from cancer last year." Or, "I completely understand. My brother was also killed in a plane crash."

I remember thinking, *They don't understand what it's like to lose a father, and no one can understand what it's like to lose my father.* I appreciated far more those who said, "I can't say that I understand, but I can relate to the tough road you're on. My father was killed last year."

Besides being "real," friends who relate are also able to feel the other's situation without minimizing it or trying to fully identify with it or attempting to "fix" it for them.

Influential

Influence is the power and authority to effectively move someone or something in a specific direction. Parents are constantly asking, "Who has my daughter's ear? I don't feel like it is me." Peers strongly influence each other in shaping beliefs and actions.

In our surveys, girls named their parents as the number one influence in their lives, with friends running a very close second. That means that we mothers are our daughters' first and foremost teachers. But it's important that we allow our girls to begin to separate from us during these preteen years. That doesn't mean we don't try to influence them. It means that instead of bucking the tide of peer influence, we recognize and accept its importance. Let's point out to our daughters the positive ways in which their friends have influenced them, and draw attention to ways that they can positively influence their friends.

Sandi's new best friend was Sophi. They did *everything* together and even traded clothes several times a week. Sandi's mom noticed that they also traded CDs, and she didn't like the lyrics she'd heard blaring from Sandi's room the past several days. One night she went in to listen. She asked Sandi why she liked that particular group. "Oh, it's not mine; it's Sophi's," her daughter explained.

The next day, Sandi's mom bought some Christian CDs that had a similar sound but offered positive lyrics. She gave them to Sandi and then purchased two tickets for great seats at that same Christian band's upcoming concert. After several days, the girls were both listening to the new Christian CDs. The old ones still come out occasionally, but not often.

Meanwhile, Sophi's mom called Sandi's mom and thanked her for allowing the girls to spend a lot of time together. "Sandi has been such a good influence on Sophi," she said.

Encouraging

Encouragement is a form of influence. Encouragement spurs us on in a direction we're already headed, or it gives us the support we need to move in a new direction. When I think of encouragement, I always think about Terri and Tanya. These two thirteen-year-olds both came from families with two kids, attended the same school, and had similar interests. But the two girls had very different attitudes about life.

Terri woke up in the morning to her mom saying, "You're late. Didn't you hear the alarm? Get dressed and be down for breakfast in five minutes." Once Terri rushed downstairs, her mom continued, "Your hair needs to be brushed; tie those shoes before you trip." After breakfast she said, "You forgot to drink your milk." Terri hurried back, drank her milk, and went out the door. Her mom ran after her. "Terri! You forgot your lunch. Bye!"

Tanya's morning began in a similar way because she and

Terri had talked on the phone together until 11:00 p.m. But Tanya's mom said, "Honey, your alarm is going off. Are you ready to get up, or should I hit the snooze button?"

Tanya answered, "Hit the snooze."

Five minutes later Tanya got up and came downstairs dressed except for her hair. Her mom said, "Great job getting dressed. All you have left to do is your hair. Oh, and be careful not to trip on your shoelaces."

Tanya tied her shoelaces and replied, "I'll fix my hair in a ponytail after breakfast."

After breakfast her mom called, "Are you finished with your milk?" Tanya ran back to finish it and then headed out the door. Her mom came running out and reminded her, "Tanya, your lunch."

"Thanks, Mom," she said and smiled. "I love you. Good-bye."

Terri and Tanya hopped on the same bus to school and proceeded to the same first-period class, where they had a pop quiz. Tanya's heart jumped, but she prayed, "Lord, help me remember what I need to know." Terri's heart sank, and she thought, *I probably won't be able to remember anything.*

Tanya noticed Terri's discouragement. She leaned over and whispered, "Think about what we studied Tuesday night. God will help you remember the answers." Tanya felt better. She needed that encouragement. Maybe she wasn't so dumb and forgetful after all!

When our daughters are encouraged at home, they will naturally be an encouragement to their friends. Often, we don't realize the tone that we are setting in the morning before they go off to school, church, or to other activities. I tend to be so focused on the goal that if we all get in the car and are somewhat on time, I feel good about the morning.

A wise mom who had raised five children of her own suggested I place a hidden tape recorder in the main part of my house in the morning. I did this and then listened to the outcome. I was pleased by some of my words, but mostly I was convicted about a few comments and my tone of voice. Try it. You will learn a lot about the climate of your family. And as you make a few adjustments, your daughter will learn some positive lessons about attitude and encouragement.

Nice

What does it mean to be nice? We've all known people who were too nice—so positive and kind that they seemed fake. But genuine niceness is an essential part of friendship. How can we pass on this quality to our girls in a way that inspires kindness and consideration for others, yet retains the ability to speak the truth in love when necessary?

In the Gospels of Matthew, Mark, and Luke, we read the account of the Lord's last supper—Jesus' final time with His disciples. Here He was with twelve men whom He knew very well, so well, in fact, that He even told them that one of them would betray Him and one would deny Him. He was willing to tell them the hard things and then demonstrate His deep love for all of them by washing their feet. Even knowing their sin, He served them in love. His actions toward His disciples were not motivated by their actions, their words, or the conditions of their hearts. Jesus was motivated by His sincere love and compassion, which deeply desired the best for each man.

Nice sounds like a superficial word without much meaning.

But it isn't. Being nice means reaching out in love to others, regardless of whether it's the bully who knocks your daughter's books out of her hand in the hall at school or the teacher who stays late to help her with her homework. Being a nice person means building deep and respectful relationships.

Paige started taking different routes to her classes because she was threatened by Patty, a big girl who had decided that Paige was just too nice and needed to be "toughened" up. One time Paige was trailing behind Patty, hoping that she would not see her, when a huge football player ran into Patty. She fell and all of her papers scattered everywhere. Several people laughed as they trampled the papers with pleasure. Paige hesitated, then stopped and helped Patty pick them up. Patty wouldn't even look at her, but when they were finished she glanced at Paige and mumbled, "Thanks."

Paige no longer needed to fear Patty, and several years later they became friends. Being "nice" simply means observing Jesus' golden rule: "Do to others as you would have them do to you" (Luke 6:31 NIV).

Dependable

The mother of Karen, my best friend in high school, told me something I've always remembered: "Friends are there for each other even when it's inconvenient." One of the greatest gifts that our girls can give to their friends is dependability. Are our daughters true to their word? Of course, situations arise that may prevent naive promises from being kept, but if the pattern of dependability and trust is established, then the exceptions will be better understood.

Bonnie had two really good guy friends, Tony and Matt,

and she enjoyed each of them for different reasons. Tony always kept her guessing. He would say, "Meet me at 4:00 p.m." Then he'd call at 3:50 and say, "Sorry, but I can't be there till six." One night she was dressed to go to dinner with Tony and his family when he called five minutes after they were supposed to leave to say they weren't going after all. Sometimes things like that happen to all of us, but with Tony it happened all the time.

When Bonnie confronted Tony, he gave her all kinds of good reasons for every incident. He felt completely justified in his behavior.

Matt was the opposite. While Bonnie could count on one hand the times that Tony kept a commitment, she could only think of one time that Matt hadn't followed through with keeping his word. If Matt said that they would meet at 4:00 p.m., he would show up at 3:55. If he was running late, he always called and apologized and still showed up.

At first Bonnie thought that the two boys simply had different personalities. But as she talked and spent more time with each of them, she came to see that Matt only made promises he was sure he could keep. He consistently tried to be there for others even if it was not convenient for him.

Tony made commitments without looking at the whole picture. He wanted to meet everyone's needs so much that he didn't meet anyone's. Bonnie now talks to Tony occasionally, but they are not close. She is still great friends with Matt even though they go to two different colleges. Friends like Matt are rare treasures. I wouldn't be surprised if Bonnie went on to marry Matt one day.

Teaching our girls to be reliable and trustworthy involves more than words. It requires us to be reliable and trustworthy ourselves. It also means that we remind them of the good, godly reasons Christians have for developing dependability.

Spiritual

"A bosom friend—an intimate friend, you know—a really kindred spirit to whom I can confide my inmost soul. I've dreamed of meeting her all my life," exulted Anne of Green Gables about her new friend Diana.[1]

As mothers, we want our daughters to have a best friend— soul mates with whom they can walk through all the ups and downs of life. Dee Brestin says in her book *The Friendships of Women*, "I would give my very life for a best friend, but I could also become as petulant as a jilted lover when a soul mate withdrew for a season."[2] She goes on to quote Gail McDonald, who says we need to ask, "Do you drive your friend to God or to you? Are your friends dependent on you or are they drawn to God?"[3]

Part of realizing each other's potential in friendship is found in bearing each other's burdens. Galatians 6:2 says, "Bear one another's burdens, and thereby fulfill the law of Christ." At different times in their friendships, our daughters will experience being the one who is weak and being the one who stands strong.

Jill and Celia were best friends. Jill's parents separated and divorced her seventh-grade year, and Jill called Celia, crying, almost every night. Celia had a hard time relating to Jill's pain because her home life was very stable, but she prayed with Jill on the phone, and God continued to give her friend wisdom and comfort. Some days Celia just needed to go over and hold Jill while she cried, without saying a word. Other days Jill needed to hear every encouraging word and verse that came to Celia's mind.

Two years after Jill's parents divorced, Celia's little brother was killed when her family was in a tragic car accident. She and her brother were twelve months apart and very close. Now Jill was there for Celia. She prayed with her, read the Bible to her, left encouraging messages on her voice mail, listened, and held her when she cried.

As our daughters' young friendships begin to take root and grow in their hearts, let's remind them that each friend is a beautiful gift, a rare treasure to cherish and love. Friends that can have fun, enjoy life together, speak the honest truth, laugh, cry, and—when necessary—face tragedy and adversity, are few and far between. I love to quote a friend of mine who says, "Friendship is not a project; it's a process that mysteriously unfolds." Let's help our daughters make sure that the roots of their friendships grow deep and healthy, so the petals will unfold beautifully as the years go by.

Moms & Daughters:
Working It Out Together

1. Talk with your daughter about her closest friends. Ask why they are close. Can she imagine still being friends with them when they are all grandmothers?

2. Write down together the qualities each of you wants a friend to have. Is she that kind of friend to others? Are you?

3. How does she handle cliques at school? What "group" is she in? Is she content there, or is she trying to move up to a more prestigious group? Discuss what she and her friends can do to build unity and acceptance among all the cliques at school or church.

4. Teach her to pray for each of her friends as needs arise. Keep track of those prayers in your journal.

11

School Influence and Grades

D o you ever get the feeling that your daughter isn't really paying attention to her schoolwork? Do you worry about her focus (or lack of focus) on learning and education, considering the countless distractions she faces every day? The truth is, she's probably a lot more concerned about her academic standing than you think she is. Out of hundreds of girls surveyed around the country, grades were listed as one of their top five concerns. In fact, 88 percent placed grades as their number one concern in life at the time of the survey.

With grades being a top concern, why is it that parents tend to see a decline in their daughters' scholastic interests? As girls enter junior high, they often feel pressure to be popular, so they focus on sports or other extracurricular activities in order to fit in and maintain a good social position. Getting good grades is often thought of as "nerdy." Peer pressure highly influences academic achievement.

In Mary Pipher's book *Reviving Ophelia*, she relates, "I saw a seventh grader who was failing everything. I asked her why and she said, 'My friends and I decided that making good grades wasn't cool.' Her story has a happy ending, not because of my work, but because the next year, in eighth grade, she and her friends had another meeting and decided that it was now 'cool' to make good grades. My client's academic situation improved enormously."[1]

In Sean Covey's book *The 7 Habits of Highly Effective Teens*, the author relates the story of a boy named Ryan.

> Peer pressure and wearing the latest style in clothes was important to me. Then I got really sick with a kidney disease, and it just seemed kind of silly to buy a bunch of clothes when in only a few months they were not the cool thing anymore. I decided that I was going to do what is most important. I started spending more time with my family, instead of being out with my friends so much, and I stopped worrying about what they thought about me, and started being myself.[2]

Sometimes it takes something life threatening to alter our perspectives on life and to reaffirm what is really important. Better we should keep talking to our girls all along the way, so that a crisis won't be a necessary "wake-up call." What does your daughter want to achieve academically? Ask her to tell you about her goals and why they are important to her. Where does she want to go to college? What kind of GPA will she need to be accepted there? How hard will she have to work to qualify and apply for scholarships? These are issues that need to be discussed before high school begins, not after high school graduation.

Parents need to remember that peer pressure is not always negative. Your daughter may be used as the catalyst for bringing positive thinking into her group of friends. Real friends influence others in a positive way, drawing them toward healthy choices. If she continues to receive unhealthy pressure about doing or being her best, it would be wise for her to step back from her present group and find some new friends who will support and affirmatively challenge her.

In Los Angeles, California, teens who are having trouble in school or with more serious matters of the law are sent to a Saturday morning "boot camp." Here they are challenged physically, academically, and socially to recognize that they have choices in the way they live their lives. As recently as ten years ago, teenagers thought they were invincible and that they could accomplish anything. Now many adolescents instead believe that they are stuck in a rut without any options except immediate gratification—most of it being illegal or promiscuous. Caring adults who get involved in these kids' lives can powerfully affect their future.

One student, Bernice Murillo, age sixteen and a sophomore at South Gate High School, said, "By the third week, I started thinking, *what do I want for my life?*" The program convinced her to stop ditching school, and she was determined to improve her grades so she could go to college.

A fourteen-year-old girl, Amy, was abandoned by her

father, her mother was in jail, and she was living with her grandmother. "I sometimes do things because I don't have my mom. I really need discipline," she explained, tears in her eyes. "I'm only 14 and I really need her. That makes me do crazy things."[3]

Our daughters need our guidance and our active influence in their lives. Otherwise, their peers will direct their thinking.

Why Worry About Grades Anyway?

Girls are concerned about their grades because they have been told all their lives that they are important. But once they show up at middle school, they don't always know how to get the high marks they once received in elementary school. Suddenly they have more teachers to relate to and their classes are generally larger. Homework is increased, and they feel overwhelmed. All of this is happening while their bodies are changing and their self-consciousness is skyrocketing.

As moms, we can sit down and discuss these issues. It's important that we let our daughters know they are normal. Yes, other girls are having the same struggles. No, they are not dumb or defeated.

Nicole was fairly good in math and had been an A/B student until sixth grade. Now, she was barely making Cs in math and she felt that if she tried really hard, she would be thought of as a "nerd." She finally told her parents that she was a C student now and she couldn't do any better. Nicole wanted to resign herself to that role rather than try to succeed.

Albert E. Gray studied successful people for years and

came up with one common denominator for success: "All successful people have the habit of doing the things that failures don't like to do. They don't like doing them either, necessarily. But their disliking is subordinated to the strength of their purpose."[4]

Nicole had a choice to make. She could take the easy road and say, "This is just the way I am." Or she could take the high road and say, "I can do all things through Christ who strengthens me" (Phil. 4:13 NKJV). Reaching for success is not always fun. It's usually hard and requires a great deal of diligence and commitment to a goal.

Although grades are very much in the forefront of our daughters' minds, they may not let us know. Or they may even argue to find a way out of the pressure they feel. This is where we can become proactive and set up enticing incentives for them to succeed, providing positive reinforcement rather than a negative reaction to their grades.

At the beginning of each marking period, write down your daughter's goals and the incentives she will receive if her goals are attained. Remind her that the choice to excel academically is hers and it must come from her own motivation, but you want to come alongside her and help her reach the goals she has set. That places you in the role of her ally, not in the position of a controlling parent, always pressuring her to do well.

"There's no excuse for your making anything less than an A," Marie's mom told her daughter. "You've always made As, and there's no reason to stop now." This mother assumed that her daughter would rise up to her demands and perform well. When the family moved in the middle of the school year, Marie's grades began to fall. Instead of talking to her daughter and trying to understand her state of mind, her mom did the opposite. She tightened the rules and raised the expectations.

On her next report card, Marie made three Fs. Her mom was shocked, but finally she realized that her demands weren't going to work. When she and Marie met with the school principal and some of Marie's teachers, they suggested encouraging her in the things she was doing right and supporting whatever efforts she made. "Grades are not the focus," they told Marie. "We just want to see you learning and doing your best."

The next quarter, Marie had managed to bring her grades back up to Cs. By the end of the year, she had an A/B average. What's more, she had regained her interest in her classes, and her natural curiosity had returned.

Marie's story is a fresh reminder about what it takes to motivate a student. Often kids feel so much pressure from their parents that they decide they can't live up to the expectations, and they give up. Or they make academic achievement such a priority that they forget that learning is the real purpose of education. This is where a mom needs to know her daughter's abilities, goals, and temperament. That way Mom can encourage her to succeed to the best of her ability! One daughter who placed grades as her number one concern wrote that she wished her mom "knew me and trusted me and didn't always try to change me and run my life!"

Mothers often talk to me about how to deal with a bad report card or how to motivate their daughters to do their best in school. I have learned a lot from a great book, *How to Talk So Kids Will Listen and Listen So Kids Will Talk*, by Adele Faber and Elaine Mazlish. The authors give a scenario of a mother talking with her son, Paul.

Paul is very worried about his math grade and lets his mom know. She first focuses on the good grades and works her way down each subject. When she reaches math, his lowest subject, she says, "Well, now, math. What do I see here? An M [minimum]. So, this is the subject you're having a hard time with?"

Paul says, "I'm going to do much better this next six weeks."

Mom replies, "How are you going to do that?"

"I'll try; I'll study harder; I'll do all of my homework and always ask my teacher for help if I don't understand."

His mom answers, "It sounds like you're setting goals for yourself. Let's get a piece of paper and write them down."

They wrote down all of Paul's subjects with the marks he received and then his goal next to it. Consequently, the focus was no longer on just math, but on improving academically as a whole. Paul wanted to take his math grade from the lowest to the highest mark. His mom questioned him, and he assured her that he was really going to work hard in math!

At the bottom of the report card his mom wrote, "I have gone over Paul's report card with him and he is going to work harder and has set some positive goals, especially in math." They both signed it, and then they hung his scholastic goals on the door to his room.

The next three days Paul came home with Es (excellent) on his math homework. His mom responded enthusiastically, "When you set your mind to something, there is no stopping you!"[5]

It's exciting to see our children reach their goals, especially when they are motivated to do so. When they become discouraged, which will happen in the process of success, remind them of Philippians 3:13–14: "Brethren, I do not regard myself as having laid hold of it yet; but one thing I do: forgetting what lies behind and reaching forward to what lies ahead, I press on toward the goal for the prize of the upward call of God in Christ Jesus."

As our daughters do their best before us and God, as they seek to learn and develop their God-given curiosity, they will bring home the appropriate grades. My sister was a 4.0 student who had lots of friends and she hardly had to study. I, on the other hand, struggled to keep a 3.25. My focus was on people instead of academic success, and it would have been a constant frustration for me to have to study nonstop to maintain a 4.0.

I was grateful to my parents for allowing me to be the girl God designed when it came to my studies, rather than pressuring me to make the same GPA as my sister. Let's help our daughters do *their* very best, and let's do our part in minimizing their fears. The more support and encouragement they receive from us, the likelier they are to achieve success in school—and in life.

Moms & Daughters:
Working It Out Together

1. Write down your daughter's current grades. Look at them together and set realistic goals.

2. Discuss her study habits and ask what works and what she would change.

3. Ask her if she feels unrealistic pressure to succeed. Let her tell you whether you are supporting her in a way that spurs her on to do her best.

4. Talk about ditching school, cheating, or having a negative attitude about school. Does she or do her friends deal with these issues?

5. If your daughter has chronic problems with reading skills, concentration, or other study habits, talk to a counselor about the possibility of learning disabilities. If necessary, have her tested.

Morality

12

In a culture where the moral climate says, "Anything goes!" many kids are looking for standards and hope. Over a decade ago, two hundred thousand teenagers gathered in Washington, DC, to set the stage for American teenagers to know that abstinence is the answer: "True love waits!" they proclaimed to the world.

Although the campaign received national attention, it was quickly passed over. When sex education became the standard procedure in the public schools of America and condoms were made readily available to teenagers, we saw teenage pregnancy increase. The numbers are finally starting to go down because of three approaches: abstinence-based education that includes facts on sexually transmitted diseases, instruction in the proper use of birth control, and abortion. In some states, a thirteen-year-old girl who wants an abortion now has the right to have the procedure done without parental consent. Even though the numbers of actual teenage births are decreasing, there is still a desperate need for the heart issues to be addressed.

Kids are naturally drawn to permissive adult influences, but they are crying out for someone to raise the standard. Out of hundreds of girls surveyed, 97 percent responded that they welcome parental and adult discipline in their lives. Kids are begging for moral absolutes. To conclude this section on the soul, let's look at some qualities that establish moral actions but flow from the heart.

Building Truth into Character

Marti Jackson was continually caught lying at school. Whenever she was asked a direct question, she either avoided it or glossed it over. This strategy had worked for her when she was younger, but now in the seventh grade her behavior was no longer tolerated.

Finally, Marti met Mrs. Cantro. Mrs. Cantro knew Marti's lying was a serious problem, and that the behavior had become so rooted in Marti's character that it was now a way of life rather than an admitted wrong. Mrs. Cantro received her first tip to the acceptance of this behavior when she called Marti's house to talk with her parents. Marti answered, and Mrs. Cantro asked for her father. A few seconds later, Marti returned to the phone and said, "My dad told me to tell you that he's not here, but he's really in the middle of a basketball game. Call back in a few hours. I'm not in trouble, am I?"

A girl's conscience is established early in life. Mrs. Cantro had another student, Shannon. She was the kind of girl who cried and asked forgiveness if she told her parents that she drank one Coke instead of two. Shannon kept "short accounts" when it came to sin because she had learned an unforgettable lesson early in life.

When she was three, Shannon took some candy from a store and put it in her pocket. When her mom found it, Shannon explained that the store owner had given it to her. With that, she started to eat the candy. Her mom called the store and found out that Shannon had stolen the candy and then lied about it. Shannon had to give the candy back, apologize, and ask forgiveness. Afterward she was spanked and not allowed to eat any candy for a week. Shannon was taught at an early age the seriousness of lying and stealing. Since then, when Shannon has lied, she has been uncomfortable. Her conscience convicts dishonest actions.

Marti, on the other hand, was in a very different situation. When Mrs. Cantro began probing, she found out that the first time Marti took candy from a store (which I have observed that most kids do at least once; I did—did you?), she lied about it, but her brother said it had been stolen. Her mom was really busy. "Just eat it," she said impatiently, "and I'll go back and pay for it later. But don't do it again," she added as an afterthought. Because of the parents' responses, the consequences of the same actions were very different. One reinforced a healthy conscience; one hardened the heart toward what is right.

In Proverbs 12:17, 19 we are told, "He who speaks truth tells what is right, but a false witness, deceit. . . . Truthful lips will be established forever, but a lying tongue is only for a moment." Truth needs to be a template for our daughters' lives and speech. As parents, we teach not only by our words but also by our actions.

"White lies" are common in our culture. They seem justified if they protect and prevent someone from getting hurt emotionally. Usually, however, they simply delay the pain. The truth eventually comes out.

Mr. Jackson could talk his way in or out of just about any situation. His daughter Marti had grown up with his example. As she went through school, her friends would marvel at the way she "handled" the teachers—all but Mrs. Canto. Finally, at her second job after graduating from college, she had a boss who saw through her tactics. He confronted her and said that people felt run over and used by her words and actions. "You'll say anything and everything to get your goals accomplished. With you, Marti, no one knows where the lies end and the truth begins."

Marti left in shock and resigned from her position. Deep down, her boss's words rang true, and after a few more jobs and encounters, she realized that she did not know truth from fiction. Years later, she came to Christ. She looks back and sees that her role models told her to tell the truth, but they showed her how to lie. Now that she is married, with children of her own, she sometimes goes to the extreme to make the truth known, and to treat with honesty and respect those whom God has brought into her life.

Integrity should become part of our lives' bedrock. When integrity is at the base of your daughter's character, everything else will fall into place. Broken trust, lying, drinking, immorality, and unhealthy friendships will no longer be threats. Integrity means to completely and honestly do what is right when no one is watching but God.

Hope was in the midst of a very challenging Bible test at her Christian school. She was usually an A student, but had struggled uncharacteristically with memorizing the verses for that particular exam. She was stuck on two passages, but then she caught a glimpse of them written on the wall. Apparently the teacher had failed to remove them before the test.

Hope strained her eyes to see. After recognizing a few helpful words, she remembered the rest of the verses. A few days later Hope received her paper back with a grade of A–. "Awesome!" she exclaimed.

Then her conscience kicked in and her excitement turned to guilt as she knew that she had not earned that grade. Hope went to her teacher and confessed that she had cheated. She should have received a zero for the test, but her teacher applauded her integrity in coming forward and just took off two letter grades. This was still a huge consequence for a straight-A student.

Hope's classmate Ellie had also noticed the verses on the wall. She had copied them and received an A on her test. This was very unusual for Ellie, who was normally elated with a C. Another student confided in the teacher that Ellie had pointed out the verses after the test. When confronted, Ellie said that she did not cheat, even though she could not quote the verses from memory. Eventually, Ellie had to visit the principal, and she received a zero on her exam.

How do we teach our daughters to have integrity? First of all, by demonstrating it in our own lives. What do we do when a clerk gives us more change than we are due? How do we handle our taxes? Do we drive with a radar attachment that allows us to elude highway patrol officers? Do we fib to our friends or relatives to avoid confrontations?

We also teach integrity by letting our girls know that, along with honesty, integrity is an essential part of our Christian character. In the book of John, Jesus often refers to the Holy Spirit as the Spirit of Truth. If God's Spirit dwells within us, we should be committed to living in truth and speaking the truth. And if He is alive in us, we will be uncomfortable when we are untruthful.

Showing Love, Kindness, and Decency to Others

We have talked a lot about love. But love involves more than talk. It is often said that love is a choice, not an emotion. It can also be said that when it comes to love, actions speak louder than words.

What is your daughter's definition of *love*? Thirteen-year-old Daria defines *love* as "the feeling you have when you know that you've done something for someone else 'just because you care' and have no other reason." Isn't that impressive?

It's an awesome thing to be loved by another person. Sometimes we take for granted those whom we should treasure the most. When a person is treasured, we go to any length to let him or her know that he or she is priceless. Although this is shown in deep and intense ways to those who are close to us, we can also reveal this kind of love in simple ways to all we meet.

Let's break down the word *love* and pull out some actions and attitudes that demonstrate love. First, we can Look *into the other person's eyes* as he or she talks to us. With children, that means getting down to their eye level. Now you are engaged in conversation. Often a look where eyes meet from across the room can give the assurance that we care and understand.

Offer a listening ear. Love listens completely, not selectively. Moms, we can be the queens of selective listening. It works fine until our kids hit preadolescence. As I surveyed girls around the country, there was a continual cry: *Please listen to me!* Are we hearing their specific requests?

"Mom, I wish you would be home more and listen to me when I have something to say!"

"Mom, I love you a lot, but sometimes I wish that you would try to understand how I feel. Sometimes I think that you don't hear my point of view."

"Mom, I really appreciate the way you ask me how I am. You listen and then take time to talk to me."

Moira, who has twin fourteen-year-old daughters, says, "If we are good listeners for our daughters, they will feel loved. Then, in turn, they will be able to exemplify love by listening to others. This is a great gift that we can give to our girls. I'm now seeing it pay off with my own."

Volunteer a helping hand, even when it is inconvenient. I often think of the good Samaritan when I ponder this idea. In Luke 10:30–42 Jesus recounts the story of a man who goes on a journey with a bag of money. He is robbed and left for dead. Two people, a priest and a Levite, pass by him and are too busy to help.

Finally, a Samaritan man sees him lying on the road. Samaritans and Jews were not usually friendly to one another, but the man takes no thought of his race. He sees the need and meets it. The Samaritan takes care of the man above and beyond any decent man's duty.

This story portrays the kind of love that we can show to anyone we meet.

A group of seventh-grade girls came up with a practical list of ways to help. It started with simply stopping and helping a classmate who has dropped her books, helping a friend when her family moves or faces a tragedy, providing free babysitting for a neighbor who really can't afford to pay, or having lunch with a lonely person. These are good starting points. Why not sit with our daughters and make a list of our own?

Finally, we can *Enrich others' lives by caring about their needs and desires*. Most people's favorite subject is themselves, so it shouldn't be hard to get them talking. Ask questions. Find out about their world. See what motivates them. What are their passions? Look another person in the eye and ask him (or her) how he's doing. "Are you having a good day?" And *hear* that person's answer. Just feeling that someone cares will brighten his or her existence.

How can we teach our daughters this kind of behavior? By modeling it for them. By doing loving things for them. By making sure they know we sincerely care, and then by putting that care into action.

It was a chilly winter evening in Houston, Texas, and my nine-year-old mind was racing thinking about all the fun I was going to have that night. Mom, my sister, and I were on our way to Jones Hall for pageant rehearsal. Every Christmas, our church, First Baptist, Houston, put on an incredible Christmas pageant. We did about twelve performances in beautiful Jones Hall, located in downtown Houston. The first half of the performance was built around a secular Christmas theme, and the second half portrayed the story of Jesus from birth through resurrection.

We stopped at a stoplight, and when I glanced into the car next to us, I noticed a grandfather and two children about my own age. As my eyes fixed on them, Mom said she would give me a penny for my thoughts.

"I was thinking about how much I love my life and I wouldn't trade places with anyone in the world!" That moment is as clear as yesterday.

Now as I look back, I am so thankful to my mom for the care she provided for me. She put her love into action in so many ways. Mom was in the choir, not because she loved it so much, but because she knew I looked forward to going on the summer choir trips abroad with my friends and I loved being in the Christmas pageant every year.

Mom made sacrifices in her own life so that I could grow through myriad experiences, including piano, tennis, ice-skating lessons, and swim team, just to name a few. Even when I went to college and was on my own, if I was performing, speaking, or playing a sport, she somehow managed to attend. Sometimes I would not have any idea that she was coming, and she would walk in, smile, and be supportive—even if I fell flat on my face. I'm very thankful for her example to me of what it means to be there for your children, and to place their needs above your own.

Upholding Christian Values

Values are grounded in our belief system. We pass them on from generation to generation, just as a relay race runner passes the baton to the next runner. It's impossible to effectively write about how to instill Christian values in our children without first looking at ourselves. I can write a book, compose articles, and speak on every national medium about raising a generation of young women with Christian values, but how I live my life at home is the greatest teacher. Yes, I sin every day and ask forgiveness repeatedly.

As for everyone else, sin becomes destructive in my life when there is a pattern—a place I keep running to in order to meet a need in a way that God did not intend. This kind of sin pattern is what we must eliminate. The bond of sin can be broken and does not have to pass from this generation to the next.

It is never too late to see God's power work in our lives. Whether it's alcohol, drugs, immorality, greed, self-righteousness, or any other ungodly behavior, the stronghold of that sin can be severed if we really want to stop.

Think of your daughter as you consider: What kind of music do you listen to around the kids? What movies and videos do you watch? How do you treat the people in your home, at work, in the community? Moms, looking at our own lives is hard, but if our lives don't support the principles we're talking about, our kids won't hear our words. What is your focus? What is my focus? Are we like the wise woman from Proverbs 14:1, who builds her house? Or are we like the foolish one, who tears it down with her own hands? I'm thinking and praying about that right now. I hope you'll take a minute to do the same.

Moms & Daughters: Working It Out Together

1. Discuss with your daughter the moral issues of lying and cheating. Write down practical ways she can learn integrity with friends, family, boyfriends, and those in authority over her.

2. Ask your daughter if she sees inconsistencies in your life when it comes to what you say and then do. If it's uncomfortable for her to tell you, draw a "safe box" where she can say anything without being judged, and ask her to write the truth and place it inside. Then deal with the issues together.

Part
III

Body

The body is, of course, the visible, physical part of our person. It is through the body that we recognize one another, making all kinds of assumptions and conclusions at a glance. But there's more to the body than appearance, and it's a valuable goal to take incredible care of the physical being God has given each of us. There are practical steps that can be taken to integrate healthy, body-honoring habits into everyday life. These healthy habits will allow the body to become the size and shape that God has naturally designed. They will also help our daughters learn to honor their bodies as God's holy temples. Let's look together at some physical patterns that can be established in our own lives and passed down to our daughters.

Body

Diet and Exercise

O ne sunny Saturday afternoon, my dad and I ventured down to the Kansas City Plaza to do a little shopping and have a father-daughter talk over lunch. I got to pick the place, and to this day I believe that the stone McDonald's on the Plaza is the prettiest McDonald's I've ever seen. Since Dad could tolerate it aesthetically, and since, at twelve, it was my favorite, off we went to McDonald's.

I ordered my usual: Big Mac, large fries, large Coke, and McDonaldland cookies. Dad had a single hamburger and ice water. (This was before salads and grilled chicken were offered.)

We chatted about politics, boys, and life. Then Dad asked if I was interested in knowing how to stay in shape without having to diet. I was vaguely curious, so I said, "Sure."

Dad proceeded to lay out a general outline of healthy eating and exercise habits that would basically eliminate everything I was gobbling down at the moment. I also could see that his suggestions would add even more activities into my already loaded schedule. I listened politely, said thank you, and moved on to another subject—probably Bruce Brackeen, my latest crush.

The next morning at church, Bruce came up to me, poked me in the stomach, and said, "You're getting a little pooch, aren't you?" He winked and walked away.

Only later did I realize that Dad had set me up by scripting Bruce's little comment about my weight. He used my crush on Bruce to motivate me.

And it worked. I went home and said, "So, Dad, what was this healthy program you were talking about yesterday?"

Dad mapped out seven guidelines for a healthy diet, brought in an accomplished dancer to show me some daily exercises to stay toned, and encouraged me to do something aerobic at least three times a week. In this chapter, I'd like to pass on what he shared with me, along with some motivators that you may be able to use with your daughter. Dad figured out mine. What is hers?

Getting Motivated to Stay Healthy

Here are some motivators shared by nine- to sixteen-year-old girls all around the country whom we surveyed:

"I like to eat healthy because it gives me energy to perform well in sports."—16-year-old

"I eat healthy—I don't let myself eat junk. Mom keeps healthy snacks instead of chips and stuff like they have at most friends' houses."—10-year-old

"If I don't eat healthy, it's because I'm in a rush. I try to eat the right foods now because I used to not eat at all."—13-year-old

"I feel good about how I look in my clothes because I eat healthy and exercise almost every day."—14-year-old

"I stay in shape because I respect my body as the temple of God."—15-year-old

These comments give us a glimpse into why girls want to be healthy. And I might add that studies have proved that becoming more fit can skim as much as twenty years off a woman's biological age, which should motivate us moms too.[1]

The two motivators most frequently mentioned by girls are sports and boys. Those are both very real to young girls, but they are not lifetime motivators. Many girls don't continue to play sports past junior high or high school. Consequently, once they enter college, their healthy habits may be left behind along with their athletic commitment. Also, once girls marry and have children, the motivation to stay in shape for their husbands may not be as strong.

Good health and fitness need to be grounded in habits that will last beyond the original motivation. This is why the goal for our daughters should not be a program or a diet, but rather a lifestyle—a lifestyle that is so much a part of who they are that it simply seems like ordinary living.

At sixteen I attended a Young Life camp with some new friends. At night we did some of those icebreaker skits that usually nailed someone (preferably a counselor) for something he or she had done or said. The third night of camp I walked in a few minutes late and observed several of my cabin mates doing their nightly "get ready for bed" routine. Then some eyes caught mine, and I suddenly caught my breath and wanted to disappear. They were imitating my evening exercise routine!

All three nights that I'd been at the camp I had taken little notice that no one else did crunches while flossing her teeth! It had become such an uninhibited and regular habit for me that I didn't give a second thought to what the others might think of me. But it wasn't all bad—by the end of the week, several of the other girls were doing crunches with me. Now, almost twenty years later, each of us is still doing them every day.

According to *Life* magazine, "25 percent of kids 13–17 called their mother their best role model."[2] That means that another lasting motivator can be our example. If we can implement healthy habits into our own lives, then our daughters will follow in our footsteps. And that doesn't mean we demand that they do what we do. Instead, our actions will prove to be stronger teachers than our words. And these actions can affect every area of life, because healthy habits established in one area will motivate healthy actions in all areas.

Just as my dad was a key influence in my life and helped me make choices that set the pattern for the rest of my life, I was very impressed with the way a young man going through a divorce handled a potentially unhealthy long-term situation to have a positive impact on his daughters' lives. Mark was going through a divorce when his two girls were ages nine and twelve. Over several months he saw his older daughter spiraling emotionally and gaining weight. Thankfully, he had a remarkably close relationship with his daughter, so they talked it through and Mark helped her get to a place where it was her own goal to get her weight under control. Together they designed a healthy food plan and a realistic exercise program.

I was curious how he motivated her, and he said his daughter received points for each goal reached. Those points could be turned in for dollars to go toward a future purchase. Together they kept a food and exercise journal, and she took up a team sport. These actions became a lifestyle, and now, two years later, Mark's daughter is still a tall, beautiful, in-shape young woman.

Mark gave his daughter an incredible gift, and in turn the process revealed his daughter's extraordinary spirit. This young woman was capable at that age to receive the gift and further build trust in the relationship with her father. As I probed deeper into the exchange, Mark revealed that it was key to identify his daughter's "moral code" and how she processes truth. His older daughter was more cautious and took a while to build trust, while his younger girl was very trusting; the younger daughter was a risk taker and often desired to jump to the result before working through the process of reaching a goal. Mark realized that it was invaluable to be close enough to his girls to recognize their individual patterns and, as a parent, be able to meet them in a place they will embrace.

Setting Guidelines for a Healthy Diet

When my dad challenged me to live a healthy lifestyle, the hardest part was giving up french fries and soft drinks. Dad said, "Go cold turkey for thirty days, and then see if you miss them."

It was hard the first week, but I was determined to reach my goal because I was definitely motivated. After a month, I went to McDonald's, expecting to reward myself with french fries and a Coke. I took one bite and one sip and realized that they tasted greasy and full of heavy, sugary syrup. Since then, I have not had fried foods or soft drinks.

Dad shared with me seven secrets to maintaining a healthy diet that would allow me to develop physically into the size and shape that God designed, avoiding the size and shape I would create with unhealthy habits. Let me share those secrets with you:

#1: Snack on Healthy Food, Not Junk Food

After school most kids are hungry. I keep an easily accessible bowl of fruit in the kitchen. My kids know that between meals they can have as much fruit as their hearts desire. Now, if I'm not supervising, some of my kids will search for something else, like a bag of chips to sneak into the den and eat in front of the TV.

When I was little, my mom had milk and cookies waiting. These are not forbidden foods, but they should not be consumed between meals. Instead, we can help by having carrot sticks, celery filled with peanut or almond butter, fresh fruit, a bagel, or live-cultured yogurt available when our daughters come home. Allow the sweets and chips only at mealtime.

#2: Drink Lots of Water

Dad sometimes reminded me, "Water is the best drink in the house!" Many believe the myth that frequently drinking water will cause bloating and weight gain. It's not true! In fact, not drinking enough fluids may slow weight loss.

In a pilot study at the University of Utah, researchers found that when participants were just slightly dehydrated, they had a 2 percent to 3 percent decrease in their resting metabolic rate—the number of calories burned when a person is doing nothing.[3] Since RMR accounts for most of the calories you burn daily, even a small drop may have a big long-term effect.

Eight glasses a day is not a joke. It's worth it, and the effects show up on your skin. Our skin needs to be hydrated as well. That's why it's a good idea to provide single bottles of water that your daughter can toss into her backpack and drink throughout the day!

#3: Eat Three Balanced Meals

The proportioned plate outlines the types and amounts of foods that should be a part of our daily diet. These foods provide the vitamins that are needed for the body to build strong bones, teeth, and fingernails, and prevent bruising, loss of eyesight, and skin elasticity.

There has been a lot of talk lately about having six small meals instead of three balanced ones. In essence, if you are snacking on something healthy at 10:00 a.m., 3:00 p.m., and 8:00 p.m., this is the same idea. When thinking about portion size, remember the saying "Breakfast like a king, lunch like a prince, and dinner like a pauper."

#4: Eat at Least Two Hours Before Bedtime

Your body does not digest food efficiently while you're asleep, leaving more of it to turn to fat. Also, you won't sleep soundly when your body is working to digest your food. If you're hungry before bedtime, drink a glass of milk or eat some fruit.

#5: Don't Add Salt or Sugar

Foods have enough salt and sugar in them already. It's wise not to add them at the table.

#6: Cut out Fried Foods

Some people have a "fried tooth" instead of a "sweet tooth." If you love fried foods, then have them in moderation. If you don't crave them but find that they occupy a good part of your diet, simply eliminate them. If food is served fried, then take off the skin. Enjoy the flavor with your taste buds, and avoid stockpiling the fat on your thighs.

Recently I read that the word *desserts* is *stressed* spelled backward. And yes, they go hand in hand. Every chocolate lover's motto is, "When the going gets tough, *eat chocolate!*" As I've surveyed girls around the country, I've learned that most of them keep a stash of sweets for those stressful moments. I keep chocolate chips in the pantry. And when I make cookies, I usually don't start with a full bag.

It's okay to enjoy dessert if we eat it in moderation. I like to reserve it for Sundays and special occasions. Just as with fried foods, if you don't crave sweets, eliminate them from your diet. It might be a good idea to do so before you acquire a taste.

Taking Care of God's Temple

Women have a way of making excuses for delaying exercise. But as Anne Morrow Lindbergh wrote, "Lost time was like a run in a stocking. It always got worse."[4] When it comes to exercise, time is usually an issue and "too busy" is the number one excuse. Girls ask me, "How can I fit exercise into my morning routine? I already wake up at 5:30 a.m. After homework at night I'm too tired. What am I supposed to do?"

Marie Anne du Deffand, an eighteenth-century French intellectual, wrote, "The distance is nothing! It is only the first step that is difficult."[5] Even when a girl's motivation is great and she can identify her fitness goal, it's a challenge for her to know where to begin. It helps to remember that a habit can be formed in just thirty days.

There are three components that work together to create a healthy body. They are a healthy diet, weight resistance, and cardiovascular exercise. We've already looked at diet, so let's break down the last two areas and see how to fit them into everyday life.

Exercise

Growing up in Houston, Texas, I had the privilege of spending time around the leading heart surgeon of the twentieth century, Dr. Michael DeBakey. As I was first starting to make exercise a priority, I remember hearing him say something like, "Your cardiovascular health depends on the habits you develop when you're young. Unfortunately, many women start eating a high-fat diet or smoking at a young age, when their bodies are able to compensate for these unhealthy habits to some extent. But as they get older and these habits become harder to break, their bodies are not able to bounce back from the damage." The memory of his words has helped me stay on track into adulthood.

Women as young as fifteen develop streaks of fat on the walls of their arteries. Fat streaks are the foundation for plaque, which can clog the arteries and eventually cause heart attacks. It's vital that we as parents lead by example with our children by incorporating healthy habits into our lifestyles that result in steady weight control and will add years to our lives.

At age nine, twelve, or even sixteen, girls aren't thinking about disease prevention. However, because we are well aware of the benefits, preventive fitness is a great gift that we moms can give our daughters. Most girls are aware of stress in their lives even as early as age nine. Consistent exercise will relieve stress naturally and give the body the energy needed to face the challenges of each day. Being fit provides the freedom to live life to the fullest. It also allows our daughters to participate in their favorite sports with less risk of injury.

After suffering a massive heart attack, my grandfather started incorporating healthy habits into his life at age thirty-nine. He lived to age ninety and, after the heart attack, enjoyed on a regular basis a life full of walking; playing golf, tennis, and handball; snow- and water-skiing; and riding horses! It's never too late for us to start making healthy habits a priority.

Aerobic exercise and muscle-toning routines are vital to fitness. When your daughter is in school, she will probably get a lot of aerobic exercise from sports and PE class. But you can help her develop this habit for a lifetime by teaching her to keep a journal of her exercise habits. She needs to have at least twenty minutes of aerobic exercise three to five times a week. If girls are playing a team sport, they are probably getting enough aerobic exercise, but even then they may see a difference in their bodies during the summer.

Girls don't usually mind making changes, and when formal exercise is not motivated by a team commitment, they can switch to a cross-training strategy. Fifteen-year-old Robin says, "I get really bored doing the same exercise, so after a week or two, I just quit and hang out at the pool in the summer. If I can do something different each time I exercise, I look forward to it, especially if I'm exercising with my friends."

Several thirteen-year-old girls who lived in the same neighborhood decided to stay in shape for the summer by getting together for power walks or meeting at one person's house and doing an exercise video. Sometimes they would play an hour of tennis or basketball at the park.

In 1996, the US surgeon general sent out a call to Americans: "Get on the move!" Since nearly half of all people ages twelve to twenty-one are not vigorously active, and because activity tends to drop drastically during adolescence, some practical suggestions were made. Washing the car, playing volleyball or basketball for at least twenty to thirty minutes, bicycling five miles in thirty minutes, dancing fast for twenty to thirty minutes, swimming laps, jumping rope, shoveling snow, and walking stairs are all ways to fit aerobic exercise into everyday life. When an aerobic workout becomes a part of their weekly routine, it will stick with our daughters as they go to college and enter adulthood.

When I was twelve, Dad gave me a daily muscle-toning routine that I incorporated into my morning and evening rituals. Since becoming a mom and realizing that time is usually short, I have condensed this custom into three simple exercises that cover every muscle in the body.

1. Crunches! Work your abdominal muscles with properly performed crunches. Raise up no higher than a forty-five-degree-angle with your hands used only for support. This prevents unnecessary strain on the back. Start out with twelve to twenty in the morning and evening and work up to twenty-five to fifty twice a day. As I said, I do these at night while I'm flossing my teeth.

2. Push-ups! After doing your crunches, roll over and work your upper body. If you do military push-ups

instead of the modified kind, you will affect the whole body. Make sure you maintain proper alignment by keeping your neck and spine in a straight line and lower your chest, not your chin, to the floor. Start with twelve every morning and every evening.

3. Squats! These can be done in the shower, while brushing your teeth, or while talking on the phone. To perform them correctly, stand upright in a balanced position and go back as if you are sitting in a chair. Make sure your knees do not extend beyond the toes. If this is uncomfortable because of a knee injury, then lie on the floor and do leg lifts (front, back, both sides).

The key to these exercises is not doing twelve, twenty, or fifty twice a day, but doing them slowly, consistently, and correctly!

Weight Resistance

When I mention weight resistance to girls, they usually envision guys pumping iron and showing off their bulging muscles. Maybe that's why weight resistance is the forgotten ingredient in some women's health recipes. Most people know how they should eat and that they need to exercise. When I talk to frustrated girls who play a team sport and eat like sparrows and yet still struggle with their weight, I can usually pinpoint why: no weight resistance!

The website everydayhealth.com notes, "Common sense tells us a pound of muscle and a pound of fat have to weigh the same, but they do differ in density. This means if you look at five pounds of muscle and five pounds of fat side by side, the fat takes up more volume, or space, than the muscle."[6] So if you take the same volume of muscle and fat, muscle will weigh more, but look smaller—thus the exercise conundrum. You may lose inches, but gain weight.

The daily toning exercises that we have discussed are a good place to start because they use gravity as resistance, but after a few months you'll need to add some additional weight. Hand weights can be purchased inexpensively, or you can use a heavy book or a dumbbell-shaped cleaning bottle to work your arm muscles. Work the biceps, triceps, and the chest muscles.

Wrist weights and leg weights can also be added while doing aerobic exercise. Isolated resistance for the leg muscles can be done with the weights while doing leg lifts for your hamstring, quadriceps, and inner and outer thighs. Weight resistance is also a key component in building strong bones and preventing osteoporosis, a debilitating bone disease.

When healthy habits are in place, there is freedom to alter them when necessary without worrying about falling into unhealthy patterns. A healthy lifestyle becomes a reality when there is already a solid foundation.

Moms & Daughters:
Working It Out Together

1. Get out your journals. Write down *everything* that you and your daughter eat for two weeks. Look at your habits. Where do you go overboard? How can your "vices" be done in moderation? One girl told me that she didn't realize she ate two candy bars every day until she wrote down her diet for two weeks. Now she has two candy bars a week.

2. Write down your daily routine for two weeks. Do this as you go, rather than trying to write it down the way you think it will be. This will help you and your daughter determine what exercise is already a part of your lives, and what (and when) others can be added.

3. Purchase some leg, wrist, and hand weights. They are not expensive. Or join a health club and work out together. Often health clubs will have some fun aerobic dance classes specifically for teenage girls.

4. Commit to doing the daily exercises together for thirty days so they will become a habit.

Weight and Eating Disorders

Jordan Ruth, my eldest daughter, has been doing daily exercises with me since she was two. When she was seven, I began to notice that she was exercising completely on her own, whether it was at bedtime or while watching a movie. I commended her and she replied, "I never want to get fat!"

When I probed, I found out that Jordan Ruth had been talking with a 350-pound woman who'd shown her the condition of her feet, which were permanently damaged because of the excessive weight she carried.

Jordan Ruth said, "I don't ever want my feet to look like that. She can't even walk very well."

We talked about how healthy habits allow our bodies to become the size that God designed. Jordan is still motivated because she's afraid of getting fat, but I'm making sure we're still talking about her reasons. Why? Because fear can be an unhealthy motivator. Fear is one of the primary causes of eating disorders.

When I was in high school, if we were concerned about a girlfriend who was looking emaciated, we might have asked, "Do you have an eating disorder?" Now, the question is raised as part of a casual chat, but it's modified. Today kids ask, "Which eating disorder do you have?"

More than eight million people in America have eating disorders—seven million women and one million men.[1] A 2010 study showed that nearly 3 percent of teenagers have struggled with anorexia, bulimia, or binge eating.[2]

Mothers whose daughters are having problems with eating ask me, "Why? What have I done to cause my daughter to feel this way?" As parents there are roles we play within the family that can contribute to many forms of dysfunction, but in my opinion eating disorders are not exclusively a parental issue.

The largest contributor to girls' unhealthy eating patterns is the media. The young women who are lifted up as role models are thirty to forty pounds lighter and three to five inches taller than their female counterparts were forty years ago. Yet women today tend to be heavier than women forty years ago. Thus today's ideal is so far from reality that it causes girls and women constant dissatisfaction with their bodies. One group of girls told me that one would feel left out if she didn't have, or didn't at one time have, an eating disorder. It has become the norm.

Anorexia and Bulimia

· ·

Anorexia nervosa—A serious eating disorder that can have life-threatening consequences. The basic components are self-starvation and extreme weight loss. The eating disorder may become self-perpetuating, giving the individual the feeling that she is in control of her life when in reality it will result in health problems, loss of self-esteem, and a sense of being completely out of control.

Bulimia nervosa—Bulimia is an emotional disorder, primarily seen in females, which manifests itself in cycles of rapid consumption of high-calorie foods followed by some form of purging (vomiting, laxatives, hours of exercise, or diuretics). The cycle is usually followed by feelings of failure, depression, and low self-esteem.

Warning signs:
- Often speaks negatively about weight and body shape
- Hides food
- Disappears after eating
- Avoids meals
- Excessive weight gain or loss
- Excessive exercise
- Uses laxatives or diet pills
- Abnormal eating habits
- Binge eating
- Fasting or extreme dieting
- Excessive checking of weight

How to help:
- Talk to the person.

- Give support—do not be critical or judgmental.
- Allow her to express feelings (remember the "safe box").
- Avoid arguing about whether she has an eating disorder.
- Give her information.
- Solicit help from family and friends.

Prevention:
- Be respectful of everyone's shape and body weight.
- Don't perpetuate the myth that being thin is the key to self-esteem and happiness.
- Avoid punishing or rewarding children with food.
- Teach children to appreciate their bodies.
- Be aware of your own prejudices concerning food, body weight, and shape.

Confidence in the Body God Has Designed

Charity was thin as a little girl. Once she started menstruating, her body began to change. She was still thin as a rail, but she had a little fat on her thighs. This haunted her; she felt that her straight-legged capri pants made her look fat. All her friends wore them, but she didn't like the way her legs were beginning to be shaped. So, she quit eating. The fat on her legs was still there, but her face looked gaunt, and when she wore a bikini, her ribs looked as if they belonged on a Third World child.

Charity thought she looked great, but she still focused on the pocket of fat. When friends expressed concern about her emaciated appearance, she just thought they were jealous. Charity still struggles and looks way too thin, but because of family and friends who care, she has finally started eating again. How did her family make a difference? Through love, support, and a lot of prayers.

Her mom did not nag her, but simply gave her healthy choices. Her dad did not say, "You look terrible." (He has admitted, however, to commenting on her thighs a few years earlier, a comment that he clearly regrets.) In the days she was struggling, he held her a lot. As she continued to eat and take care of herself, he'd often say, "You're becoming more beautiful every day."

Our bodies should look the way God designed them to look, not the way we envision. One of the key messages of the Girl Power movement is "You can be anything! Visualize yourself as a certain size, profession, athlete, etc. It can be accomplished!" This assumes that a young girl knows what to visualize. When she sees a five-foot-nine-inch, 109-pound girl in her mind, we have a problem.

We need to talk to our daughters about what is beautiful. What size are your daughter's bones? Are they petite, small, medium, or large? How tall is she? What is the recommended weight for her height? These are all questions to address. And if we don't do it, our girls will be seduced by the media images that are thrown at them hundreds of times a day.

When a girl has an eating disorder, she cannot see her body image clearly. It is a tragedy when a girl wastes away physically, deceived by the lie that her body is fat. The following excerpt, from my book *Fit to Be Mom*, tells the story of just such a tragedy:

A 1994 article in our Nashville newspaper *The Tennessean* entitled "Starving for Perfection" underscored the danger of appearances. The focus was on "a young gymnast who lost her life because she thought she had to reduce to a size 0 in order to attain the 'Perfect 10.'" This young woman, who was twenty-two, died after succumbing to bulimia and anorexia. At the height of her career, she weighed ninety-five pounds. When she died, she weighed only sixty-one pounds. Christy Henrich's death jolted the gymnastics world, but it should be a wake-up call for all of us. The article challenged parents: "We cannot afford to let our children believe that they will be perfect if they lose weight. In fact, we cannot afford to let our children believe they need to be perfect!" This powerful statement is applicable not only to children but also to women from adolescence to adults of all ages.[3]

What Causes Eating Disorders?

My friend Marcia shares a story about her daughters, who are eleven and fourteen.

My oldest daughter arrived home from school talking about an assembly on eating disorders. She said to me, "I'm glad that you're not a controlling mother because that was the main thing to watch for, and I basically had all of the other warning signs." We had a great talk and I knew that an eating disorder was not an issue for her, but I started to be aware of the behavior of my other daughter and recognized that she was a perfect candidate.

She and I began to talk and I could tell she was hesitant to share openly. So, I drew a box. I told her that it was a safe box where she could write anything. She wrote words that confirmed my suspicions but also let me know that we had caught it in time. I still see the tendencies, but we are communicating. I've started giving my daughters a massage once a week. This has become an ideal setting for sharing our hearts with one another. I'm so grateful to the Lord for allowing my eyes to be opened before it was too late!

God certainly gave Marcia wisdom in dealing with her daughters. Eating disorders stem from emotional needs going unmet. Often a family like Marcia's will have a middle child (she also has a younger son) who allows his or her voice to be known through a symptom like an eating disorder. When a mom has several children, sometimes it's hard to recognize that one child's needs are unmet when the others are doing so well. When a child's emotional needs are not satisfied, she will interpret that as rejection. Thus her tendency will be to find comfort in food. This will be especially likely after an episode in which she has felt rejected. This results in compulsive eating, bingeing, or bulimia.

Each of our daughters needs to feel nurtured, accepted, secure, and competent as a person and within her relationships. If this doesn't happen, she may react by wanting to control food. If she feels that her life is out of control because someone or some set of rules is controlling it for her, then she may choose not to eat—the beginning of anorexia. This is her way of saying, "You can tell me what to wear, where to go, and what I can and cannot do, but you can't make me eat!"

Most girls have a deep need to please people. This can

result in taking unhealthy measures to become what they think other people would like them to become. In particular, a male role model's comments can have a huge effect on a girl's response to this issue.

Emma had two daughters. Linda was very thin and Lisa was overweight.

Emma's father, the girls' grandfather, was always complimenting Linda, the skinny daughter, and passing down her grandmother's clothes to her, since she and her grandma were the same size. Lisa, the heavier daughter, received comments like, "You had better get some exercise!" "Don't eat that dessert," or, "I saw a nice outfit for you, but it didn't come in your size." Grandpa thought these would be helpful motivators, but instead they were destructive words that left Lisa powerless. They tempted her toward an extreme response to food, which would enable her to gain control.

Emma could feel Lisa's stress about her weight, and she decided to go on a diet with her daughter. They started together with a healthy eating and exercise plan. The first week Lisa lost five pounds and Emma lost nothing. By the end of the first month, Lisa weighed twelve pounds less, and others were beginning to notice. Emma, who had lost less than two pounds, was great moral support, but she was also becoming aware that Lisa's eating habits had been reduced to a carrot, a few bites of yogurt, and water.

As Lisa rapidly lost the weight, her self-esteem started to soar. Guys were flirting with her; she was suddenly getting all kinds of attention from the same boys who had once noticed only her sister. She was able to wear Linda's clothes, and her body looked fit because Lisa was now up to running three miles a day. But at this point, she couldn't stop. Life was finally turning around since anorexia had become her partner. Because of the immediate gratification of her habit, Lisa could not see that she was on a destructive path. More about Lisa later, but first let me tell you about another girl's battle with food.

Theresa lived with her mom, who was divorced and had a new boyfriend every few months. Often Theresa would find herself confronted with one of them in the middle of the night. Usually she warded them off, but several times she could not, and she finally gave in to their sexual requests. At first Theresa felt guilty, but she liked the attention because it came from someone who was interested in her beautiful mom. Then one night, she had a scary and painful experience with one of these men, and she left home to live with her grandmother. She never told her mom why. Theresa knew that it would make her disappointed and angry.

At her grandmother's she was loved but had little, if any, emotional support. When Theresa felt lonely, angry, tired, or sad, she learned to find comfort in food. Food became the friend that never let her down, and as she gained weight, she felt that food had also become her protector. The heavier she got, the less anyone would want to violate her. She had come to the conclusion that if she looked undesirable, men would leave her alone.

After Theresa had gained more than fifty pounds in three months, a friend at school confronted her. But this only served to make her deceptive. She made a point of eating more sensibly at lunch in order to please her friend, while hiding food in her backpack to consume throughout the day. As far as Theresa was concerned, food was her salvation, both comforting her and keeping her safe. She could not see that her "ally" had become a cancer that was destroying her from the inside out.

Can you see some of the thought processes that drive girls with food addictions? Does any of this make you wonder about your daughter's condition? As with any problem, the first step is to recognize that there is a problem. This means beginning to see the disorder as an enemy, not as a friend. For moms, that means communication. And communication, especially in a case like this, means learning to listen with our hearts as well as our ears.

Our children know when we hear them or when we're just going through the motions. We need to listen with our whole beings, and we need to make sure that they receive one response, loud and clear: "You're important!"

When I was sixteen, my mom, dad, Young Life leader, and friends thought I was doing great. I was popular, and I had the "right" boyfriend, car, grades, clothes, and everything else I could dream of. I loved pretending to be the young woman everyone thought I was. I didn't want anyone to find out there were some holes in my armor. I was strong and confident and always seemed to make the right decisions.

When my dad died the next year, I had to begin facing what was really on the inside. I realized that I didn't have to be perfect and always have all the right answers. I needed to trust God and the people He'd placed in my life. I would have continued to move along in a very destructive pattern had God not allowed tragedy to intervene. My path led me to convince everyone around me that I was wonderful, and I would have continued until I finally hit some breaking point down the road.

Moms, let's take the time and trouble necessary to look behind our daughters' facades. And let's help create a *real* world in which they can honestly and genuinely grow up to be moral, godly, successful, and happy women.

Some girls will go to any length to convince Mom that all is well, when inside they are crying out for someone to see their pain. As we have discussed, some girls will be more overt in their efforts to get our attention, but generally those with eating disorders have perfectionist, controlling personalities and will simply insist on maintaining an image. Many times we won't see the pattern until it has advanced. We need to watch carefully.

And there's no harm done if we ask the key questions and find that we are wrong about the eating disorder. Then the talks will still have served a good purpose in building a closer bond for open communication. As we open up new levels of communication, let's remember Marcia's story about drawing a safe box. A safe box or a safe conversation is a place for our daughters where anything they choose to say will never be used against them. If we violate this once, even if it seems to have been for their good, trust will be broken.

But suppose you aren't wrong. Suppose you determine that, yes, there is an eating disorder. When the problem has been identified, what is the answer? Giving advice, making strict rules, and requiring your daughter to change her habits will only push her farther away. The first step is to continue to listen and ask questions that will bring her to her own conclusion of why this behavior is destructive. How is she feeling? What is the problem? What can be done to solve it?

Keep asking these questions, especially if "I don't know"

is a consistent answer. Timing is important. Don't beat the talk into the ground and therefore close the door for another more open discussion. Use wisdom and really *hear* what she is saying. When she tells you something, use your own words to say the same thing back to her, so that it's clear that you're listening and understanding. The purpose of your conversation is to unearth the deeper issues. There is no easy answer or quick fix, and it's important for us to grasp this truth: *An eating disorder is a symptom of a spiritual problem. When the heart is transformed, the disorder will be healed.*

Let me share with you the outcome of Lisa's story. Lisa had a tender heart toward God. She knew something was wrong, but she couldn't identify the problem. She and her mom had always been close—until the last few years. But now Emma sat down with her and lovingly asked strategic questions. It took a week of probing, but Lisa finally saw that anorexia had become her enemy.

Emma knew that they were headed toward healing when Lisa said, "At first I thought I had finally figured out the way to be popular and accepted. People were drawn to me, and I knew that it was because I was becoming thin. It was like I'd found the 'best-kept secret,' and I didn't understand how it could be wrong. Then, when everyone said I was too skinny, and I started fainting and being too tired to do fun things with my friends, I began to see that anorexia was ruining my life. It was taking away everything that was important to me—my friends, my health, my favorite activities. And now even my family was disappointed in me." For Lisa, anorexia was no longer an incredibly wonderful secret. It had become a terrible, uncontrollable sin.

She's Twelve Going on Twenty

Emma told Lisa that she loved her, and she did not shame her for her sin. *Sin* simply means missing the mark of perfection. Try as we may, none of us are perfect, and all of us are sinners. Romans 3:23 says that *all* have sinned and fall short of the glory of God.

Finally Lisa asked, "How can I stop?"

This is a constant challenge, but remember that in Christ we are "a new creation; old things have passed away; behold, all things have become new" (2 Cor. 5:17 NKJV).

Lisa got on her knees with her mom and asked forgiveness for her sin; forgiveness for having her emotional needs met through controlling food rather than through an intimate relationship with God. As she spent time in God's Word and talked with other girls who faced a similar struggle, she began to embrace God's unchanging attributes and to find her acceptance and security in Him. Lisa still struggles with anorexic tendencies, but there is consistent victory. If she starts to obsess about being fat, she looks at pictures of how thin she was and reminds herself how very unhealthy and sickly she had become.

Girls are not always as ready to work through their sin as Lisa was, but we need to be patient anyway. Love and understanding go a long way, and we must remember that they always come *before* a solution.

Neither you nor I have the ability to change, heal, or rescue our daughters. God must do this in and through them, and they must be willing to open up their hearts and allow Him to work in their lives. A change of heart will bring about an emotional shift from the addiction, to God. And that shift will bring about lifelong change.

Moms & Daughters:
Working It Out Together

1. With your daughter, make a list describing an ideal young woman: how she looks, what she does, and why she looks the way she does. Discuss your daughter's perception of female beauty and focus her attention on the uniqueness of every person.

2. Both of you write down your "best" and "worst" physical qualities. Are the ones that are frustrating changeable (weight, hair, etc.)? Or are they aspects of the way God has designed you (height, feet, nose, etc.)? Discuss positive ways to change the qualities that can be altered. Thank Him together for the ones that can't be changed. Reread Psalm 139 and also read 1 Corinthians 10:12–13.

3. Draw a safe box. Explain its purpose and ask your daughter if she would like to write something in it that she's previously had a hard time sharing. If she says that she doesn't have anything to write, place paper in a place that is accessible to her. Tell her if she ever needs to write anything, it's there for her, and you will be there to listen.

She's Twelve Going on Twenty

Drugs and Alcohol

Abusive drinking and drug addiction are dangers to both men and women, both for the harm they do to the body and for the dangers they cause to others. It is estimated that alcohol is a factor in 40 percent of all crime,[1] and in 2007, 26 percent of the victims of violent crime reported that the perpetrator appeared to be under the influence of alcohol or drugs.[2]

Most teenagers who abuse alcohol or drugs are not addicts. They are simply curious about the thrill. And this isn't a very wise form of curiosity: the desire to achieve an altered state of consciousness can lead a relatively healthy kid to make some pretty sick choices. As mothers of young girls, we have an opportunity to intercept that curiosity and confront it with facts before our girls find themselves in the midst of a dangerous encounter.

Helena grew up in a conservative home and had never had more than a few sips of wine when she entered her sophomore year of high school. She had a good group of friends. Some were a little wilder than others, but her parents felt good about the companions she chose.

One of the girls outside of Helena's intimate group planned a slumber party. Helena's parents allowed her to attend, and she was looking forward to hanging out, popping popcorn, and watching old movies, which is what she'd been told to expect at the party. But when she arrived, there were already a few guys there, and they were drinking beer. She found out that the girl's parents were out of town and that her twenty-year-old brother was in charge. She knew very well that she wasn't in a good situation, but she was too intrigued to leave.

Helena had a glass of wine and began feeling more comfortable. She sat down with a group that was smoking marijuana, and her curiosity increased. Finally she tried it. It made her feel high, relaxed, and carefree. Helena had noticed her hostess's brother, Bret. He seemed older and more mature than the other guys at the party. Soon the two of them were talking. He seemed to say all the right words, and something about him touched her heart. Her guard began to come down. Helena had always dreamed of dating someone in college. Soon she and Bret were making out on the couch.

The next thing she knew, Bret was carrying her upstairs. She told him that she liked making out, but sex was not an option. He said, "Okay, you have my word. I just want to have some privacy and get away from all those kids. You really stand out because you're not only beautiful, but obviously more mature than the other girls."

Helena felt safe after Bret gave her his word. But before long, because of the effects of the wine and the marijuana, she started drifting in and out of consciousness.

When Bret locked his bedroom door, Helena became scared. At first he was gentle and sweet. But little by little, he began to explore. "No! You promised," she said as emphatically as possible.

The next thing she remembers was looking up and seeing him standing naked in the bathroom. She looked down and realized that she was naked too. Horrified, she covered herself and screamed, "You raped me!" When she threw a shoe at Bret, he shut the bathroom door with a smile.

Once Helena began to return to her senses, she got herself together and left. An eighteen-year-old girl took her to the hospital to be examined. They faked a medical release from her parents, and Helena chose not to call the police because she didn't want her parents to know that she drank, did drugs, and was raped. She did not speak of the incident to anyone until she finally confided in the counselor at her Christian school. Only then did her healing process begin.

Today, as Helena looks back, she realizes that curiosity led to her actions. She wishes she had felt the freedom to express her questions at home. But above all else, she knows that her behavior was rooted in the intentions of her heart. Although God has done a great work in Helena's life, and although she clearly knows the effects of drugs and alcohol and does not want to experience either again, she will carry the consequence of so foolishly losing her virginity for the rest of her life.

Building trust with our daughters is a vital part of our

relationships with them. Part of that process is found in educating them about the dangers of drugs and alcohol. Of course, the choices are theirs, and as parents we cannot control all the actions of our teenage children. Still, there are steps we can take to lovingly protect our girls. Let's look at some preventive measures, at what to do if a problem already exists, and finally, at the answer that brings healing to the struggle.

Making Risks Known and Understood

Helena learned the hard way that drugs and alcohol put people at risk. Does your daughter know how these mind-altering drugs can affect her? Walk her through the effects of using and drinking. And while you're at it, try to help her understand that these habits often lead to other abusive behaviors. Here's what happens.

First, her brain will become baffled, and she will not be able to pick up on the warning signs around her. Her judgment gets messed up so that she can't make the wise decisions that will keep her safe.

Second, when in an altered state, it is hard to fight back. The natural, God-given adrenaline designed for our protection instead brings about an uninhibited state. This state of mind will allow her to take risks without feeling fearful. Eventually, if she passes out, as Helena did, she will be utterly defenseless.

Third, she may find herself in physical danger. A recent survey shows that 39 percent of guys believe it's okay to force a girl to have sex when she is stoned or drunk.[3]

Booze and Your Body[4]

• •

Drinking a lot does more than get you drunk—it can kill. Here's a summary of what happens at different blood alcohol levels (BAL).

BAL: 0.02
EFFECTS: After only one drink, you feel mellow, talkative, and less inhibited.

BAL: 0.05
EFFECTS: You might feel giddy and less alert. Judgment and self-control are weakened.

BAL: 0.08
EFFECTS: Your muscle coordination is all messed up. You're thinking less clearly and are less able to make rational decisions.

BAL: 0.10
EFFECTS: You are legally drunk in most states. Reaction time is slowed, and balance and coordination are out of whack. It only takes a 100-pound girl about two drinks to reach this point; a 140-pound girl, three drinks.

BAL: 0.15
EFFECTS: Your speech may be slurred, you may be stumbling and off balance, and you feel very disoriented and dizzy. To others, you're obviously drunk. You'll reach this point after four drinks.

Drugs and Alcohol

BAL: 0.30

EFFECTS: At this level, you have a lot of trouble standing or walking. You may vomit as your body reacts to the large amount of alcohol in your system, and you may pass out. (To reach this point, Susanna, about 115 pounds, probably had the equivalent of about eight drinks.)

BAL: 0.40

EFFECTS: Total loss of consciousness. Breathing slows and may stop. Body temperature lowers, and you could go into a coma or die.

• •

What About Her Friends?

Jane's mom and dad divorced when she was eleven. Her mom remarried a man who seemed wonderful, but he soon started verbally and physically abusing both mother and daughter. By the time Jane was thirteen, she had met a girl at school who lived on her own and made it sound inviting. She left a note to her mom that said, "Mom, I love you, but I have to go. You think you love Jim, so you can't see how bad things are at home. I hope you will see someday. I'm not mad, but I have to go. I'll call you when I have a phone number. Love, Jane."

Jane was unusually mature emotionally and physically for her thirteen years. She quickly learned survival strategies so she could go to school, work, and get by on her own. After a few months, she became ill with the flu and felt lonely and confused. For the first time she missed her mom. She called her and left a message about where she was and said that she was sick. Her mom never called back.

After that disappointment, Jane went into a depression. A neighbor brought some beer over one night, and she began to acquire a taste for it. Soon she was experimenting with hard liquor and various drugs. These substances made Jane feel temporarily better, but her life was a mess. No longer did she have any goals. She had lost her sense of direction.

What led Jane to this downward spiral? Most of our daughters and their friends don't face such an extreme situation as hers; however, deeply felt unmet needs are present in everyone, especially in adolescents. Some leading contributors to emotional crises are divorce, grades, social pressures, stressful home life, moving, relationship breakups, or the death of a parent, sibling, or a close friend. These stresses trigger a teenager's desire to escape. Drugs and alcohol seem to offer a place where, even for just a while, she can feel better and experience a sense of well-being.

A young girl's deepest longings are for love, acceptance, and security. These qualities may be present in the home, but perhaps they weren't communicated in a way that reached her heart. When parents see the symptoms of substance abuse, it is time to look at the climate of the home. Parents are never entirely to blame for their children's actions, but sometimes those actions amount to a cry for help. If so, a close look at the needs behind the actions can bring healing in areas of our lives that we don't see or have chosen to overlook.

If You Suspect Alcohol and Drug Abuse

It is a tough, painful experience to learn that your child has been involved in some form of substance abuse. The first step any Christian parent can take is to seek wise counsel. "Where there is no guidance the people fall, but in abundance of counselors there is victory" (Prov. 11:14). Search for other parents who have walked this road with their children. If possible, learn from their mistakes as well as their successes.

First, *identify the problem.* "Teens who start abusing alcohol or drugs at an early age are at much greater risk of developing an addiction later in life compared to those who misuse drugs later," says James Garbutt, MD, a professor of psychiatry at the University of North Carolina at Chapel Hill and a research scientist at the Bowles Center for Alcohol Studies.[5] Parents and close adult friends need to be aware of the red-flag occurrences that may prompt such behaviors (as identified in the preceding story about Jane) and warning signs, such as suddenly acquiring new friends, and address them immediately. Now, many kids live in single- or two-career families. Often by the age of twelve, a child becomes a latchkey kid who takes care of herself in the afternoon. This leaves little time for adult supervision.

Moms, our children need adult role models who care. This is especially true if you're a single mom. As we've seen before, girls respond to wholesome male attention from their fathers, grandfathers, or some other father figure. If there is a lack of male influence in your daughter's life, then she will naturally look to fill that need in other not-so-wholesome ways. Try to find a godly male adult who will spend time with her. If you don't know where to begin, ask God to guide you, and talk it over with a pastor or youth leader at your church.

If her father travels a lot, go before the Lord and ask Him to fulfill this need. Then watch the amazing way God provides positive male involvement through relatives and family friends. It's also exciting to watch God work out her father's schedule so that he's there for the vital occasions where his presence is sorely needed. God has a way of working out the details of our lives, but He often waits until we ask for His help.

Once the problem is identified, *acceptance* must follow. As parents, we have the ability to push our children toward the sin or to draw them away from it. We can place a million rules and boundaries on our daughters, but if they do not feel loved and accepted in spite of their sin, they will rebel.

Even if love and acceptance are demonstrated, your daughter will usually not consciously realize it until the healing process begins. The next step is to commit to *walk through it together.*

Carol had been drinking and using drugs since eighth grade. She went to the youth group at church and had some older friends there who showed her how to cover up her habits. Her wealthy parents loved her, but they were busy, distracted, and self-absorbed. They chose to overlook the evidence, even when several hundred dollars turned up missing from their safe. Carol's nanny was busy with the younger children and saw Carol as little more than a helper to her.

Finally, during her sophomore year of high school, Carol was arrested at a downtown club. Her parents' first impulse was to bail her out, but a wise friend advised them to let her stay overnight and face the consequences of her actions. Carol had bragged to the others that her dad was a wealthy, influential businessman who would make sure she was bailed out in a matter of minutes. She was stunned when her dad said, "Sorry, Carol, but you're going to have to spend the night there. Your mom and I will be praying for you, and we'll see you tomorrow. In the meantime, I hope you'll use this time to think about your actions."

For Carol, the night in jail and a sentence of forty hours of community service were enough to wake her up and motivate her toward change. Today she credits her parents for the way they handled that situation. It was the alarm that woke up the whole family and required them to face the unhealthy environment in their home.

Change is hard. Most people don't really want change, even after they recognize the problems they are facing. Sadly, it is often the plight of our children and the behaviors they display that alert us to the broken areas of our home life. Once we are confronted, we are ready for change, no matter how hard it has to be. But although changing behavior is a start, true healing cannot take place without a change of heart.

Bringing About Lifetime Change

In Isaiah 55:6–11 we are given the answer to changing our lives once and for all:

> Seek the LORD while He may be found; call upon Him while
> He is near. Let the wicked forsake his way, and the unrigh-
> teous man his thoughts; and let him return to the LORD,

and He will have compassion on him, and to our God, for He will abundantly pardon. "For My thoughts are not your thoughts, nor are your ways My ways," declares the LORD. "For as the heavens are higher than the earth, so are My ways higher than your ways, and My thoughts than your thoughts. For as the rain and the snow come down from heaven, and do not return there without watering the earth, and making it bear and sprout, and furnishing seed to the sower and bread to the eater; so will My word be which goes forth from My mouth; it will not return to Me empty, without accomplishing what I desire, and without succeeding in the matter for which I sent it."

Here, God lays out the steps for putting the desire for change into action. The steps are:

1. Seek
2. Repent
3. Forgive
4. Worship
5. Rest
6. Growth

First we must *seek* the Lord. Cry out to Him for help! Stacy was determined to become a cheerleader. She was a part of the "druggie" crowd, yet she had always dreamed of cheering in high school. The summer before tryouts, she tried to quit doing drugs. She set a lot of rules for herself and really tried to stop. When a friend recognized her struggle, she shared the gospel with her, and Stacy became a Christian. She faced the usual withdrawal symptoms and needed to be involved in intense counseling and accountability. But because of her quest for God, her desires and her lifestyle began to change.

Stacy's second step was to recognize her drug abuse as sin and *repent*. True repentance asks for forgiveness from God and from others who have been affected.

Only after that kind of repentance could Stacy *forgive* herself. Many girls are comfortable asking God's forgiveness, but they cannot let go of the weight of their sin and forgive themselves. Lack of forgiveness leads to guilt, anger, and bitterness, while forgiveness is a turning point in the healing process. First John 1:9 says, "If we confess our sins, He is faithful and just to forgive us our sins and to cleanse us from all unrighteousness" (NKJV). If He has forgiven us, how can we refuse to forgive ourselves?

Once we have confessed and received God's forgiveness and cleansing, we must recognize how incredibly great our God is and truly *worship* Him!

This leads to peace and *rest*, something the drug addict or alcoholic has not experienced, and cannot.

Then the lifelong process of continued *growth* begins. The foundation of effective growth is found through spending time in God's Word. The Bible is a powerful book written by the living God through men. It has the ability to penetrate hearts and lives and to accomplish God's purposes in even the most broken heart.

Moms, in the midst of the difficult years of our daughters' adolescence, our examples speak the loudest in our homes. As we try to implement these principles, we may first want to look at our own habits and go through these steps in our own lives. It may or may not be drugs or alcohol for us, but we may discover other unhealthy habits that need to be weeded out of our hearts and minds. As we work on ourselves, our daughters will be watching. Let's make sure they learn from us that, although all behaviors can be modified, it is only after God changes our hearts that we are able to maintain a healthy lifestyle for a lifetime.

Moms & Daughters: Working It Out Together

1. Discuss the effects of drugs and alcohol with your daughter.

2. Talk about her habits and her friends. Does she or do they struggle in this area?

3. Set standards together about how she will respond when tempted to engage in drugs or alcohol.

4. How is she feeling now toward drugs and alcohol? Is she curious? Is she giving you the "right" answers while still wanting to experience the thrill for herself?

5. Read Romans 5–6 and discuss grace, obedience, and the freedom we have in Christ.

16

Sex and Purity

In our recent survey of girls aged nine to sixteen, many of them wrote, "Mom, I wish you knew what happened between me and my boyfriend." The greatest moral dilemma they reported facing was the battle to maintain sexual purity in their relationships with the opposite sex. As noted in a previous chapter, although we have seen a decline in teen pregnancy rates over the last five years, it appears that the availability of birth control, rather than a commitment to abstinence, has been the leading contributor to this decline.

And abstinence isn't a popular subject on television, on the Internet, or in teenage magazines, not to mention in conversations with older, more experienced kids. If it hasn't happened already, our girls will soon be confronted at least three times a day with the issue of premarital or extramarital sexual activity. At some point their consciences can become numb to the harmful impact of intimacy in an inappropriate context. In popular culture, sex outside of marriage is portrayed as the ultimate act of love, the one clear sign that two people really mean a lot to each other. If we don't do our jobs in telling them the truth about sexuality and purity, our daughters are going to be confused and vulnerable. And ultimately, they will be seduced.

Becca asked to talk to me after experiencing sex for the first time with her boyfriend. She read to me from her journal entry because it was too hard for her to say the words aloud.

Becca wrote, "Months of being strong and finally my passion overruled my control. I imagined the most incredible experience like the ones described in the smut magazines I often read when Mom's not watching. It was exciting and an unforgettable experience, but it was awkward and afterward I felt dirty and cheap. Like a used coffee filter that should be thrown away. It wasn't at all like the movies. I guess that's why they cut away before the two are finished. It takes so much emotional energy to deal with the aftermath of a few moments of fun."

As I speak with girls around the country, their stories of sexual adventure always seem to produce somewhat the same results. Sex is not love. People have tried to tell them so—pastors, youth workers, teachers, and—yes—their moms. Yet today the lines have become so blurred that even Christian young ladies who have been taught the truth sometimes try to justify their inappropriate actions in the name of love. To complicate matters, these situations sometimes happen simultaneously to girls and their single mothers, who are living out the life of dating after divorce. The following example shows that maturity and experiencing the "knocks of life" sometimes lead to wiser choices.

Brent, a single dad, and Emily, a single mom, had a solid friendship, but there was a definite attraction between them. One night, after blending their families for a cookout, "that moment" happened and they wanted to kiss. They had had a lot of honest conversations, and both knew they weren't ready for a commitment and didn't want to hurt each other or risk the friendship. Here they were, in this perfect, spontaneous moment, *so* wanting to kiss, but they hugged and left.

Later they went to coffee and talked about honor. They both admitted to being "in the moment" and acknowledged that they were still not ready for a commitment. A kiss would have been fun, but it probably would have parlayed them into a romantic relationship way too fast. It was worth passing up the opportunity to kiss in order to respect each other as a brother or sister in Christ and honor God first and foremost while providing protection and preserving friendship. Now they kid that it would have been fun to just kiss, but they also know how cool it was to take the tougher path, because honor was finally more important than meeting their desires of the moment.

The Greek word for honor means "to value." When we show honor, as Brent and Emily did that night, it shows what we value. We guard and protect what we value, and we hold those we value in high esteem.

So do we tell our daughters, "Don't kiss"? No! Kissing is one of the most incredible interactions God created to take place between a man and woman. Let's say with our words and show with our actions that it's worth it to wait for the right time, when kissing is flowing out of an already established, committed relationship focused on honoring God and each other. If this standard is our hearts' desire and guides the way we are in relationships, then we will most likely kiss men who seek first to honor God, then to show us honor. These men will value and treasure us once we are "caught." And prayerfully, by the grace of our Lord Jesus Christ, we will also first honor God and then honor our men. In doing so, we value our mates in the way God has designed, not allowing them to become idols. If we will look to the Lord and wait on Him, then kissing will work out at the right time and be more than worth the wait. Whatever happens it will be best—God's best!

Do you remember your own struggles? I do. If we're honest, most of us have held in our hands the double-edged sword of wanting to do what is right yet yearning to fulfill our passion. Now our girls face even graver consequences for sexual promiscuity than we did. Pregnancy isn't necessarily the number one fear anymore. The threat of STDs (sexually transmitted diseases) can be a motivation for purity, yet it is not the answer. Let's look at some of the facts we can use to equip our daughters, and let's consider some practical tools that will assist them in making wise choices.

Facing the Dangers of Sexual Promiscuity

There are approximately 34 million people infected with HIV worldwide,[1] and between 2002 and 2020, AIDS will be responsible for an estimated 68 million deaths.[2] While condom use decreases the transmission of AIDS and gonorrhea by between

50 percent and 100 percent, studies examined by the National Institute of Health in 2011 showed that condoms may not be nearly as effective against the spread of other STDs. And STDs such as herpes and human papilloma virus can be spread by skin-to-skin contact in areas that condoms don't cover. For these reasons, Dr. Tom Fitch, who serves as the board chairman for the Medical Institute for Sexual Health, advocates abstinence or monogamy, although he does not discourage condom use.[3]

Laura found out about the threat of STDs after she accepted contraception from her high school nurse. "I'll take them just in case things get out of hand with my boyfriend," she said with a shy smile. She knew pregnancy was not an option, and she realized that it was the only thing stopping her from giving in to her boyfriend's advances.

Laura's mom had always told her to wait until she met "the one" she truly loved. "It will be worth it," she had said.

The experience wasn't exactly what Laura had dreamed about, and after suspecting a bladder infection, she was diagnosed with a type of STD that may be with her for the rest of her life. And she lost her virginity in the process. Laura might have restrained her passion a little longer if she had understood the risks. Her boyfriend had only been with two other girls, but Laura learned from experience that old lesson: when you have sex with someone, you are also sleeping with all the women (or men) in the person's past.

The fear of getting pregnant often keeps girls from intercourse. Still, in a compromising moment, passion usually wins over purity. Cissy found this out the hard way. She gave in one night, then broke up with her boyfriend the next day. A month later she discovered that she was pregnant. Her father was a pastor, and her family was well respected in their suburban town.

Cissy confided in an eighteen-year-old friend, who took her to get an abortion. Cissy was sad but felt that this was the right choice. "What kind of life will the baby have anyway?" she told herself. "This way it won't be an outcast. Besides, it will go straight to heaven."

What Cissy was not prepared for was the traumatic experience of hearing and feeling her baby being sucked out of her body. She could not forget the sound of the vacuum or the tears of the other girls who were also ending their pregnancies. Shamed and sorry, she told no one, and the friend who helped her moved away. Two years later she was still preoccupied with her aborted child and haunted by flashbacks and nightmares. Finally, Cissy went to a counselor and confessed. The healing process began, but she will always carry the weight of having decided to destroy another life.

Consequences such as STDs and pregnancy are not an issue within a godly marriage. When two healthy people marry and remain faithful, they will never need to worry about the risks of sexually transmitted diseases. And babies are God's gift, not an unwelcome disruption, to a couple who honor God. Marriage is God's means of sexual protection for His children.

Learning to Understand and Respect Their Bodies

Next to grades, relationships and sexual purity are primary concerns for our daughters. The decision to stay sexually pure has to be made before temptation arises. We can begin educating our daughters by helping them understand their own bodies. As early as four and five, girls begin to explore their bodies and ask questions. Dr. William Slonecker says that parents need to teach their children the proper names for each body part and encourage them to state their questions openly and honestly.[4]

When a young child is fascinated by a private area of the body or makes a sexual gesture, it is important to keep open the door of communication. Children who are told, "Don't touch that; don't talk about it," will eventually act out in inappropriate sexual ways.

From an early age our girls can understand the purpose and function of their mother's breasts. Missi's nine-year-old daughter asked her, "What are those for, Mommy? And why don't I have them?"

"They are a beautiful and private part of a woman's body," Missi explained. "They are used to store milk to feed your baby. Also they are for your husband to enjoy someday." Missi explained by quoting Proverbs 5:18-19, which says that God planned for men and women to be exclusive in their love for each other: "Rejoice in the wife of your youth . . . Let her breasts satisfy you at all times."

Her daughter also asked, "What does my vagina do? Why does blood come out when girls have their periods?"

Missi answered, "The blood is stored in the body in case you have a baby. When a woman is not having a baby, the blood comes out of her body. The vagina is also a private area of the body only to be shown to Mommy or Daddy if you are hurt or taking a bath, or you can show it to Dr. Johnson. It's also the part of the body that God will use someday for you and your husband to make babies."

These questions are natural and can be answered in a way that will help build a proper moral foundation. Candor and frankness in the early years prepare for openness and honesty during adolescence.

Besides knowing about the inner workings of their bodies, girls also need to understand how a woman's body responds to a man. We need to help them understand that just because the body is "on fire," our human will can choose not to respond. In Jesus' time, girls married at age twelve or thirteen, and that's why our daughters are so ready for sexual experiences. Our culture says to wait to get married, and our Christianity says to wait for sex until marriage. Waiting for both is the right decision, but the drives still exist. And our girls are now more susceptible to sin because birth control is so prevalent. Sex is accessible and seemingly without consequence.

When our girls are taught to recognize a guy's intentions, they will be better able to keep healthy boundaries (which we will discuss later) when a sexually charged encounter takes place. They need to understand how boys' bodies work, and how intensely they are driven toward gratification if they aren't committed to God's ways. And a girl also needs to be secure in the fact that if a boy doesn't respect her enough to honor her limits, then the relationship is in serious trouble.

In 1 Corinthians 6:17–20, Paul wrote,

The one who joins himself to the Lord is one spirit with Him. Flee immorality. Every other sin that a man commits is outside the body, but the immoral man sins against his own body. Or do you not know that your body is a temple of the Holy Spirit who is in you, whom you have from God, and that you are not your own? For you have been bought with a price: therefore glorify God in your body.

As a Christian, your daughter is one with the Lord. It is inconsistent with God's morals for her to become one with anyone else until God joins her together with a man of His choosing in marriage. Also, her body is not her own. It is Jesus' gift to God. We are living inside this temple that God designed, and we need to bring glory to His name with our bodies.

Let's help our girls see how valuable they are to God. Your daughter's body meant so much to Jesus that He paid for it with His very own blood. When she respects her own body this way, she will attract the guys who have the self-control and the confidence in Christ to make wise choices. That doesn't mean they won't struggle. It does mean that the struggle will end God's way.

Two Excellent Examples of Wise Choices

Joseph

I love the story of Joseph and Potiphar's wife. This story is found in Genesis 39 in the Bible. Joseph was a man of excellence, integrity, and obedience. Potiphar was Joseph's boss, and he often traveled away from home. Potiphar's wife had her eye on Joseph; she felt profoundly attracted to him.

Joseph was a good-looking, successful man, and Potiphar's wife longed to have sex with him. One day, when her husband was away, she said, "Joseph, lie with me."

Joseph refused. He said, "Behold, with me here, my master does not concern himself with anything in the house, and he has put all that he owns in my charge. There is no one greater in this house than I, and he has withheld nothing from me except you, because you are his wife. How then could I do this great evil, and sin against God?" (vv. 8–9).

Well, the woman may not have been much else, but she was persistent. And Joseph's strength of character probably enticed her even more. Finally, after he continued to refuse, she grabbed at him as he fled, and his garment remained in her hand. She then accused Joseph of making advances to her, using the garment as evidence. Infuriated that his trust had been betrayed, Potiphar threw Joseph in jail.

Even in jail the Lord had favor on Joseph, and "whatever he did, the LORD made to prosper" (v. 23). Eventually, of course, he was set free, and he became the second most powerful man in all of Egypt.

Regina

Regina isn't a Bible character, but she has a heart for God. A few years ago, she had a huge crush on T.D. He was a handsome football player, the most popular boy in school. He seemed to have a lot of girlfriends, each thinking she was his favorite, but everyone knew "That's just T.D."

T.D. started flirting with Regina in Spanish class. He also began taking roundabout routes to his classes so they would run into each other. Somehow he sensed that she was special, different from the others. She knew all about his reputation and was determined not to become one of his "girls."

After a few months, T.D. began coming over to Regina's

house after school to "study." She realized that she was starting to really like him. Somehow she found herself wanting to talk to him all the time. Finally he asked her out on a date. She was excited but apprehensive. She didn't know what to expect.

She talked to her mom and asked what to do if he tried to kiss her. Her mom laughed. She said, "Kiss your finger and place it on his lips and say, 'Save it—it's worth the wait.'"

Regina went out with T.D., and at the end of the night, he parked the car before they reached home, and he leaned over to kiss her. She did as her mom had suggested. T.D. pulled her close and said, "No girl has ever refused to kiss me."

She pulled back and he grabbed her and tried to French-kiss her.

She slapped him and demanded that he take her home. When they arrived at her house, she got out of the car and said, "I enjoy your friendship, but until you can show me the respect I deserve, I can't speak to you again."

Of course, T.D. was floored by a woman who could be so strong. He went and talked to his priest, who told him that he had to change. He admitted to sleeping with just about every popular girl at his high school. Somehow he kept all of them happy and didn't get caught because each thought that *she* was his one true love. He said that he had finally met the girl he wanted to marry and asked how he could get her.

T.D. started attending a Christian parachurch group on Tuesday nights, but he still couldn't give up the girls. They were less frequent, but it was a constant struggle. Then, at summer camp, he recognized his sin and asked Jesus into his heart. As he began to grow, his lifestyle started to change.

Regina kept up with him through a friend. She couldn't figure out why she still felt so close to him.

One year after their first and only date, T.D. called Regina and asked if he could see her. After they'd talked for a while, she agreed to meet him at a restaurant. He was truly a changed man. She could see it in his eyes, hear it in his voice, and recognize it by the way he spoke to her and treated her when they were together. They dated for the rest of the school year and all through college.

Because sex was such a weakness for T.D., they waited until they were engaged even to kiss. They married three months later. T.D. later wrote, "Regina was like an angel sent to wake me up to the fact that I was on a destructive road. Then God rescued me and created a new man who was able to truly love God, myself, and others. Surrendering everything to Christ has given me the peace that I had searched for my whole life."

God gave Regina the strength to withstand T.D.'s advances. But her mother gave her the right advice at the right time. And Regina respected her mom enough to listen to her.

Facing Sexual Temptation

Regina had made up her mind not to give in before she was confronted with the opportunity for physical gratification. When I talked with her about her experience, she said that staying pure was a continual struggle. She remembered the first time her eyes met T.D.'s, the first time he touched her arm and "electricity" shot through her. At times her body ached for his, and had strict boundaries not been set, she could not have resisted the temptation.

The main reason for Regina's purity was that she trusted God and His Word. Regina believed that God would not have designed sex solely for marriage if it were not in her best interest. Deuteronomy 24:5 says, "When a man takes a new wife, he shall not go out with the army, nor be charged with any duty; he shall be free at home one year and shall give happiness to his wife whom he has taken."

God is *for* sex in marriage! Regina's parents studied the story of Joseph with her, and from that they developed four "Don'ts" and four "Dos." Let's take a look at their guidelines.

Four Don'ts

1. Don't get into a compromising situation. **Talk with your daughter about what are and are not appropriate situations to be in with a guy. Help her understand rules such as: "Don't be in a house alone with a man." "Don't go into his room or let him into yours with the door closed." "Don't go to a hotel room alone with a guy." Be proactive so that the temptation is not an option. It may sound like a bunch of killjoy legalities, but if she can see the whole picture, she'll understand. Your daughter needs to be convinced that with the right man—the man God chooses for her—she will experience it *all* for a lifetime. Then it will be worth the wait and the needed self-control.**

2. Don't be deceived by persistence and persuasion. **Girls need to understand that even nice guys have some great**

lines. Sometimes they are just testing a girl to see if she will give in. This can be especially true when a guy wants to find "the right one." He will sleep with the girls who give in, but he wants to marry the one who doesn't. Some typical lines are, "Kissing is harmless. What could be more innocent?" "I'll make love to you now and I'll make love to you when we're married." "Making love is another way of saying, 'I love you.' It's a lover's language." And on and on. Educate her on lines and lies. Many guys will determine a girl's dream and become that for her. She must be able to stand her ground and not let him persuade her to compromise.

3. Don't let down your emotional boundaries. **The emotional connection is the most vulnerable door to a physical relationship. When a man can look deeply into your soul, the physical will soon follow. Encourage your daughter to set emotional boundaries that will not allow him in completely until he has earned that right to her heart. It bears repeating: "Guard your heart, for everything you do flows from it" (Prov. 4:23 NIV).**

4. Don't be confused by overpowering feelings. **It's easy to lose sight of your standards in the heat of the moment. This is why Joseph ran. He knew that if he lingered, he might be pulled into trouble by his passion. We need to let our daughters know that even a look can send the body to a place of passion. It will be hard for her to think clearly, especially when she thinks she is in love, or when she has resisted for so long and now just wants to experience the forbidden. The answer is *run*!**

Four Dos

1. Be consistent in your relationship with God. **Spend time in prayer, reading and memorizing Scripture, and hanging out with Christian friends.**
2. Confront the possibilities. **Recognize the temptation and figure out how you're going to deal with it. Have a game plan. The sin is not in the bait; it's in the bite.**
3. Consider the consequences. **Any sin can be forgiven, but sexual sin is not only against God, but also against the immoral woman's own body. This carries huge consequences, which we have already discussed.**
4. Flee first; think later! **Joseph did not ask questions or try to reason with his seductress. His actions cost him his job and his reputation and landed him in jail. Yet God knew the truth, and He worked out everything for good, just as He's always promised to do. Decisions made with integrity are never regretted.**

Modeling Behavior for Our Daughters

Jody is a beautiful woman who finally married again as her daughter graduated from high school. She said it was a tough challenge to be divorced through her daughter's teenage years, because she and her daughter both were being pursued by men. She shared that this stage of dating again reminded her of the first time around, and now that her daughter was watching, she decided to do things differently. Jody said that when a man pursues a wife, he often wants a conservative girl who has kept herself for her husband. Although she was a virgin when she married the first time, she had been an "everything but" girl—what she thought was the Christian way to honor God and not give up much, to get and give what a girl wants without compromising and still glow with innocence on her wedding night. But now she didn't want her daughter to do the same.

When her daughter turned twelve—right after Jody had divorced—Jody gave her a purity ring. After a time of healing, Jody realized she needed a purity ring too. She said it was clear as day that God was calling her to seek Him to restore her virginity—not in the technical sense, but in the emotional sense—and to walk forward in that commitment. Jody acknowledged that even kissing was a huge temptation when a woman has already experienced the gift of sex! Jody admitted that the "everything but" way was a counterfeit action that appeared to honor God but was actually just a different way to serve self. Her decision to be radical (according to the world's standards) in the way she related to men was an incredible testimony to her daughter and kept the line of communication between them open. Jody shared that her daughter liked the fact that she (Jody's daughter) was different, but with every new year she wondered why she needed to wait when everyone else doesn't do it that way anymore. Her daughter later confided that often the path of honor seemed impossible, but she would think, *If Mom can do it in her forties, I can wait too.*

So where is the balance? Sometimes a kiss happens; sometimes it leads to more. Does this mean we should give up? Just like our daughters, we will have consequences to our actions. Some are weak in this area, and some are not. Some feel called to celibacy, and some constantly struggle with unfulfilled desire. Today is a new day. We are moms with beautiful daughters, and some of us are now single. God can restore the virginity we once had—not technically, but emotionally—and we can reclaim our reverence for Him and our commitment to walk in obedience. God has given us grace; give grace to others, pray for each other, and hold each other accountable. Let's go humbly before the Lord on our knees each day, seeking to walk today in a way that honors Him!

The desire to have self-control and integrity in our relationships must come from within. It is an area that, depending on whether we ask Him to, God either does or does not control. When God is in control of our minds and hearts, our wills and emotions, we will still sin, but we will not walk in habitual sin. And we can always start over, no matter what we've done.

No matter how many unwise choices your daughter has made, help her understand that she can be completely forgiven, able to stand clean before God. In Christ, when we confess our sins and Jesus forgives and cleanses us, we are able to start over as new creations. No matter what may have happened in the past, your daughter can step proudly into the future, a pure virgin in God's eyes. For with Him, nothing is impossible.

Moms & Daughters:
Working It Out Together

1. If you haven't had "the talk," now would be a good time!

2. Take her to a store to buy supplies for when her "time of the month" arrives. Also, purchase a training bra so she will have it when she needs to wear it.

3. Ask your daughter what boundaries she has or would like to have with guys. Share some of the ones that you had when you were dating.

4. Talk about how you handled temptation before marriage. If you struggled, tell her about your regrets and your need for forgiveness from God. But a word of caution: girls sometimes justify their immoral behavior, saying, "Well, Mom said she messed up, and she's fine now." Don't leave her with the idea that it was okay for you to fail. And even if you're talking about the terrible consequences, providing all the details of the sin will do more harm than good.

5. Talk through scenarios that could come up with guys, and role-play how to handle their advances.

6. Listen, listen, listen! Your daughter may have questions she's been afraid to ask. And she may have things to tell you that she's been afraid of letting you know.

17

Style and Body Language

Blake was excited about her first date with Jeff. Even though it was a group date and Jeff's dad was driving, she couldn't believe her parents had said yes. At school she day-dreamed about what she would wear, and after her homework was completed, she started trying on outfits. She rummaged through her closet, all her sister's clothes, and her mother's, but still, *nothing*. Finally, she decided to buy something new with the money she had saved from her summer job.

She found some cute jeans, a formfitting T-shirt, and some thong platform sandals. Blake asked her mom on the way home, "Why is it that I have all of those clothes in my closet, but when there is something special coming up, I can't find anything to wear?"

"Oh, that's normal, honey. A girl feels pretty in something

new, especially if she has saved her money for it. However," she said, "there are smart ways to make an old outfit seem new by using accessories." They talked about buying a scarf, the "perfect" shoes, or a piece of jewelry that makes an already-owned outfit unique. They talked about finances and how to spend money wisely when it comes to style. Girls sometimes go overboard in this area, and Blake's mom was wise to teach her how to put limits on style. Someday, Blake's husband will be thankful for their conversations.

What Blake wears on her date will also communicate her sexual attitude and availability. Some girls dress in a seductive way and then say they won't even kiss. Our daughters' style of dress needs to be consistent with their character. Style provides the first impression they make on others, and body language sets the level of communication. Although what clothing is "in" and what is "out" will change every year, the principles are still the same. Let's look at some guidelines that we can pass on to our daughters.

Clothes That Send the Right Message

Caroline attended a weekend junior high camp where a former Miss America was speaking. She talked about how to dress, walk, converse, and organize. This was good, but the part that Caroline remembered later was about dress. Caroline's parents had given her a strict dress code. She was not allowed to wear tank tops with skinny straps or tight-fitting pants that were "in." She had always thought her parents were just boring and old-fashioned.

Then the speaker said, "When you dress, dress for Jesus." At first, that sounded a little silly to Caroline, but it stuck with her. She began to judge her clothes by how she would feel if she were wearing them and ran into Jesus face-to-face. For example, since formfitting clothes were the style, she learned to put a sweater around her shoulders to take attention away from her chest. She taught herself how to dress in style, yet to dress modestly. Her parents were proud of her choices and soon gave her full freedom to pick out her own clothes.

Encourage your daughter to dress with her own flair. She doesn't need to look like everyone else or dress in some way or other that Mom thinks is cool.

Paula and Katy were best friends, and they had a similar way of dressing. Their friends gave them a hard time because at least once a week they would both show up at school in exactly the same outfit—and they never planned it that way. Your daughter will naturally dress in styles like her friends', but it will be good for you to help her learn to make her own choices within the appropriate guidelines. Show her how to focus on her physical assets and see which styles look best. She doesn't need to dress in the latest style all the time. It's important that she feels comfortable and that she looks good in her clothes.

Anna's dad was out with her one night, and they saw some of her friends from school who looked gothic and wore makeup like vampires. He asked them, "Hey, what's up with this Halloween dress in July?" They were surprised by his interest. Usually parents whispered about them and kept their kids away.

Since he showed genuine interest, they said that they were

into darkness and death. It was cool to be a part of the dark side. These were agreeable, seemingly normal friends of his daughter's who were trying to find an identity in the way they dressed. Anna's dad was able to talk to them a little about their philosophy and to raise some important questions without being judgmental. In a similar sense, it's important that we as moms don't condemn our kids when they express disturbing trends through dress. We need to focus on bringing out what is in their hearts. What's the motive behind the material?

Accenting the Natural

I have always admired Grace Kelly, not only because of her natural beauty and acting ability but also because she maintained a realistic and balanced perspective while being "Princess Grace." Though she lost her life suddenly in her prime years, Grace Kelly remains forever intriguing.

As an economic adviser and author, my father had the opportunity to develop many wonderful and interesting friendships. One evening he sat next to Grace Kelly at a dinner party. During the course of their conversation, he related the challenges of having two almost-teenage daughters. He mentioned his special concern that my sister and I already thought we were almost twenty, especially in the way we dressed and in our insistence on wearing makeup. Princess Grace's response was unforgettable: "My rule of thumb is that a girl can never go wrong if she accents the natural beauty God has given."

This was definitely something that Dad passed on to his daughters. I started to notice that the girls whom I thought were really pretty were not just the ones who looked older. I was drawn to the girls who *enhanced* their God-given features through makeup rather than letting makeup dominate their faces. Soon, for me, blue and purple eye shadows, thick mascara, and bright lips were replaced with natural eye shadows and blush, light mascara, and a natural lip gloss.

Most girls are frustrated about some part of their appearance, whether it is hair, eye color, or height. I love the story of Amy Carmichael. As a little girl with big brown eyes, she prayed for blue eyes as bright as the ocean. She had been taught about faith from her Christian parents, and she strongly believed that God would answer her persistent prayer.

Well, Amy's eyes didn't turn blue. Her mom explained that God had designed her for a very special purpose, and for that she needed brown eyes. When Amy became an adult, she was called to be a missionary in India. To have an effective impact on the people, she needed to look like them. She darkened her skin with coffee grains and, with her large brown eyes, the Indian people thought she was one of their own. During her years in India, God used her mightily; she rescued girls from being temple prostitutes and discipled many of them.[1]

The Lord knew the purpose for Amy Carmichael's life long before she was born, and He fashioned her physical appearance to fit her calling in life. As her mother did so well, we can help our daughters understand that God has a special purpose for their lives and has molded them both inside and out to fulfill that mighty work in them.

Accenting the natural is a valuable motto even when blemishes appear and refuse to go away. It's amazing that they are still a source of frustration even into our twenties and thirties.

Swollen eyes and redness, unsightly rashes, and sallow color are sometimes causes for insecurity about our appearances. Whatever your daughter's dissatisfaction with her face, it will look a lot better if she finds a way to apply a light cover rather than piling on a gallon of makeup. Of course there are special times for dressing up and looking glamorous, but even then we should enhance, not attempt to remake, our appearances.

And that brings us to another important point—teaching our daughters about good skin care. You can help your daughter immensely by finding a quality product for her face that matches her skin type (it need not be expensive) and by showing her how to wash, tone, and moisturize her face and neck every morning and every night. When formed early, good skin-care habits, like habits of exercise and diet, will last a lifetime.

Recognizing the Power of Body Language

We communicate our intentions within relationships not only through the way we dress and make ourselves up but also through the way we act. Eye contact is the first form of body language, but what follows can determine the level of intimacy between two people.

The head can show whether a person is determined (straight forward), curious (tilted to the side), relaxed (tilted backward), or defeated (tilted down).

The face communicates the person's mood—whether she is stressed or just "hanging," tired, or ready for anything.

The shoulders portray whether a person is tense (shrugged up) or comfortable (naturally down).

Arm position tells a tale about a person's state of mind. Arms by the side speak of self-assurance; arms folded in front show self-protection; arms behind the back show great confidence.

If hands are pointed out, they put the focus on the other person; if pointed in, they put the focus on the self.

Leaning against a stable object with feet crossed demonstrates a relaxed comfort in the situation. Or maybe the person is just tired. If the other person leans forward, it is a surefire signal of interest—unless he or she is leaning toward you in anger.

While becoming aware of what their body language is saying, girls also need to set standards about how they will hug a guy. A full-frontal, close-to-the-body hug should be reserved for intimate relationships. A side hug or a "loose" forward shoulder hug is the best way to say hello without communicating anything inappropriate.

Holding a guy's hand lets him know the level of comfort in the relationship. Our daughters need to recognize that even this action is a high honor, and a guy should take each step into physical affection slowly and thoughtfully.

Body language is a powerful tool, often used by boys and girls to communicate unspoken intentions.

Laurie was talking with a good-looking boy at the dining room table after they had finished studying. She was warm, so she took off her jacket and then propped her foot on the side of his chair. The next thing she knew, he was leaning forward to kiss her. She was startled but quickly kissed him back. Later when they talked, he said that he knew she wanted him to kiss her because she had taken off her jacket and put her foot on the side of his chair. She was not consciously trying to open any doors, but she had hoped he would kiss her one day. It just happened more quickly than she expected.

Most of us have learned about these things in bits and pieces along the way. But the world is becoming more complicated every day, and our daughters are longing to know all they can about how things work and what things mean. They will deeply appreciate our input on these issues, but they may not know how to ask the right questions. They may not even know what questions to ask. Why not turn the page, and we'll work together to find some helpful answers?

Moms & Daughters: Working It Out Together

1. Get out some teen magazines and let your daughter show you the styles she likes. Discuss them and agree on what is and is not appropriate dress. Then *go shopping*! (Just tell your husband or money manager it was part of your assignment for this week!)

2. Talk about makeup and hairstyles. Look at pictures and discuss what you see and like.

3. Create a plan for your daughter's skin care.

4. Discuss the different aspects of body language and what certain gestures and movements can mean.

5. Work together to create guidelines regarding body language. Our daughters should not be naive in this area.

　　　　　She's Twelve Going on Twenty

18

Boundaries

When Maxfield, my eldest son, was two, he often went charging toward the fireplace and climbed up onto the hearth so he could look closely at the fire. It didn't take him long to discover that climbing up there would bring about a big, emphatic "No!" from Mom or Dad. He was allowed to look at the fire only from the edge of the hearth. Now and then guests watched him moving toward the fire and became concerned, but I didn't say anything. I always kept my eye on him, but I knew that Maxfield had learned his boundary.

A study was done years ago, observing schoolchildren during recess. The researchers found that if there was not a fence around their playground, children stayed in the middle of the schoolyard, not venturing far afield. When a fence was present, they ventured out to the fence line and enjoyed the entire play area.[1] Boundaries gave them—and give to us—freedom, because they provide a sense of safety.

Boundaries are healthy, and our girls begin learning (or not learning) about them at a very early age. In property issues, fences define where one person's turf ends and another's begins. In relationships, boundaries are much the same. A boundary is a nonnegotiable line that lets another person know that he or she can go so far and no farther. And it implicitly means that inappropriate or abusive behavior that violates the boundary will not be tolerated. Men and women of integrity do not cross other people's boundaries.

Girls who learn to set boundaries physically, emotionally, and spiritually are at a clear advantage in life. God has designed healthy limits for our protection, and He expects us to stay within them and to keep others from violating them.

In Hosea we read the story of Gomer, who leaves her husband, Hosea, and becomes a prostitute. In Hosea 2:6, the Lord says, "Therefore, behold, I will hedge up her way with thorns, and I will build a wall against her so that she cannot find her paths." God placed a boundary around Gomer, and if she tried to cross it to pursue prostitution, she would be hurt and unable to find her way. Boundaries not only help us overcome sin patterns, but they also keep us out of trouble in the first place. Let's take a look at some guidelines we can share with our daughters for setting boundary lines in our relationships with others.

Establishing Physical Boundaries

When I was fourteen, my family and I ran into a distant relative in the airport. This man took me in his arms and gave me a very close and intimate hug. I thought that he was excited to see me and didn't feel especially uncomfortable since he was a relative of some sort. But afterward, Mom pulled me aside and said that I should never let anyone but intimately close family hug me in that way. She explained that even men who seem safe should not be allowed to embrace me that closely.

On the other hand, I loved holding hands with my granddaddy, and if I sat close to him, he'd put his arm around me and hold me close. My grandfather respected godly boundaries, and he was a safe person for me.

All females need to receive physical affection from males. It's best if Dad is the one who provides this affection for our girls, but if he is not available, then a close family member who really loves them could meet the need. It is when that need is not being met that girls go "looking for love in all the wrong places" and are vulnerable to sexual abuse.

Physical boundaries need to be clearly understood. One out of every four women will be battered at some time in her life,[2] and 32 percent of women raped are between the ages of eleven and seventeen.[3] How can we protect a beloved daughter, as best we can, from becoming a statistic? It all goes back to boundaries.

We need to set physical standards with her, especially when it comes to relationships with the opposite sex. Some key questions need to be asked and answered: When is it all right to hold hands, hug closely, or kiss? Where will the line that says, "This far and no farther," be drawn? You and your daughter can and should talk about these principles long before they are put to use in a practical way.

Even when standards are established, it's easy to forget them in the midst of temptation. During the last decade, many teenagers have become aware of the importance of abstinence, and even guys are proudly calling themselves virgins. Part of the reason for this is that concerned parents have been taking life-changing weekend trips with their daughters.

Angela had known since she was little that the first weekend after her eleventh birthday was reserved for a trip with her father. Her dad, Greg, surprised her and took her to a bed-and-breakfast in a quaint town nearby where they could canoe, fish, and go for long walks. At dinner Saturday night, Angela's dad pulled out a small box. It had a pretty locket inside containing a picture of her and him.

"It's beautiful!" she said, pulling it out of the box.

"Before you put it on," he said, "give me a minute to explain what it means. This locket is a reminder of the promise that you have made to God to remain pure until marriage, to save yourself physically for your husband.

"Every time you choose to hold a guy's hand, to hug closely, or kiss, you are inviting him to move closer to you. All of these steps lead to the final act of intercourse, which should be saved for your husband.

"As you wear this locket, remember that you are a delicate flower to be given completely to only one man. When you meet him and desire to marry him someday, God will give you an overwhelming peace. Mom and I will also know that he is the right one for you, and he will have respected you enough to wait for you to give him the gift of yourself on your wedding night.

"Any guy who doesn't care enough to show you this kind of respect is not worth dating. Will you promise me that you will wait for the right man? The one that God has chosen for you?"

After Angela answered yes, her dad fastened the locket around her neck. He said that he would add another locket to her chain with a picture of her and her husband on her wedding day. Although at eleven, Angela did not quite realize the significance of this gesture of love, she fully understood it when she walked down the aisle, a beautiful virgin with two golden lockets around her neck.

Angela had many frustrating nights when she had to walk out of tempting situations. And at times things probably went farther than she had anticipated. But the standard had been put in place, the boundary established for her protection. As a result, she was able to give the gift of her virginity to her husband. I pray that this will be my daughter's story too. Don't you?

The young men who are actively seeking God with their lives look for this moral code in the girls they pursue. Greg shared that this is why as the relationship builds, it's key to allow time to cultivate the emotional connection, especially if there is physical attraction. As Greg unraveled his hopes for a relationship and told me about the married men he spoke with who looked back at what they desired and forward to what they hoped for their sons, there were several constants:

- There is time to explore the values and vision of the young woman that a man is getting to know.

- The young woman waits for the man to move things forward and lets him be the one to ask the "where is this relationship going?" question when he's ready.
- The young woman is able to be real and doesn't hide behind outward attributes, like lots of makeup or being in perfect shape; instead, she has balance, both inside and out.
- The young woman is committed to wait for marriage before the man has complete access to her intimately. However, all the men Greg spoke to said that it's seldom that a guy will turn intimacy down if it's available and the woman desires to give it away.

Greg ended our discussion by saying that in general, these qualities are desired by all guys. It's a moral code, but one that's often overlooked because men take advantage of the fact that many girls in this generation are "easy." Men really desire a challenge. Girls who maintain physical boundaries may be surprised to find that men respond with respect, rather than frustration.

Understanding Emotional Boundaries

Physical boundaries are not overstepped without reason. It is our emotions that cause physical boundaries to be broken. Girls who have gone too far physically have told me that the hardest part to walk away from afterward was the emotional bond that had been formed. When a girl gives herself physically, she has also allowed the young man to penetrate her emotional life. Many marriages suffer because of emotional abuse, and even when physical boundaries are not overstepped, emotional damage can be imposed in both word and deed.

For years, we've tried to teach our little girls to find a healthy balance between expressing and suppressing their emotions. But in adolescence their emotions often swing too far in one direction or the other, and we have to start all over again, teaching them how much is too much.

At fourteen, Judy wears her feelings on her sleeve. She is quick to tell you of her troubles and talks constantly about herself. It frustrates her that she does not have many, if any, true and long-term friends. Since most people pull away from her after a few months, she then clings to them by calling or showing up unannounced. Her emotions are high when people respond to her positively, but they run very low when she feels them pulling away.

Judy has not learned to establish emotional boundaries with people. She is drawn toward people that make her feel better about herself, especially beautiful and famous people. A perfect example of Judy's type of personality is found in the sister of the leading male character in the movie *Notting Hill*. She is very needy, and when she meets Julia Roberts's character, she clings to her and says that she hopes they can be best friends. It is a hilarious moment, perfectly portraying the "Judys" of this world.

My mom taught me a valuable lesson when I was twelve. As I battled with friendships, boys, and grades, she said, "Before you go to anyone with a problem, take it to the Lord first. You can always tell me anything, Kim, but if you want to share what is on your heart with someone else, pray about who it should be—maybe one or two people—then don't say anything to anybody else. Most of your friends don't want to hear about your frustrations, so use your words wisely!"

This nugget of wisdom has helped me ever since. Of course we should be honest about ourselves when asked, but even then we don't need to bare our souls to everyone. I love Proverbs 17:28: "Even a fool, when he keeps silent, is considered wise; when he closes his lips, he is considered prudent."

We have previously discussed healthy emotional relationships. In friendships, it's important to encourage your daughter to see if her friendships are mutual. Do she and her friend equally call each other? Do they both enjoy spending time together? Is there a healthy emotional exchange? Is she able to be herself in her friendships, or does she take on other identities? These are questions to examine and discuss with her to determine if healthy emotional boundary lines are in place.

Does your daughter tend to become emotionally dependent? The emotionally dependent person tends to allow another person's life to feed her own. Because of this dependency, when any distance forms between her and the other person, she feels emotionally crippled. In this type of relationship, there are no boundaries. The burdens and the joys of the other person's life become her own, and she has a hard time separating herself from the other person.

Let's help our daughters understand the dangers of innocently getting too close to the wrong person emotionally. This certainly includes texting and social media encounters. Emotional dependency of any kind can destroy her focus, defeat her goals, and distract her from the calling God has on her life. If she is struggling in this area, or if both of you are battling this issue, then give it some time—time away.

Time is the ally of healthy relationships. An emotionally unstable person who is ignoring all natural boundaries will demand to deal with a person on his or her own terms. An emotionally healthy person will give others time to sift through a tough situation or deal with a loss. Providing time out is a loving gesture. It allows God to begin the healing process.

Another important emotional boundary is drawn between mother and daughter. It bears repeating—sometimes we moms tend to live vicariously through our daughters, thus stifling their individual growth and development. This kind of relationship not only stifles the daughter, but it shipwrecks Mom when her daughter packs up and leaves for college. The opposite can also occur, where the daughter is so dependent on the mother that she wants to live at home, attend a local college, and never move out. Both scenarios need intervention so that the mother and daughter can have an emotionally nurturing relationship.

Overcoming unhealthy dependencies requires a true change of heart that only God can perform. Proverbs 2 is a powerful chapter. I call it the "if and then" chapter of wisdom. God promises that *if* we will receive His sayings and treasure His commandments, *then* we will "discern the fear of the LORD and discover the knowledge of God" (v. 5).

If we "cry for discernment, lift our voices for understanding; *if* we seek wisdom as silver and search for her as for hidden treasure; . . . *then* we will discern righteousness and justice and equity and every good course. For wisdom will enter our hearts and knowledge will be pleasant to our souls; discretion will guard us; understanding will watch over us!" (vv. 3–4, 9–11, paraphrase).

Our daughters need to learn, as soon as they are old enough to understand, that when emotional boundaries are continually broken, only the power of God and His Word are able to bring about genuine change. When God's truths are sought with the fervor of a mother searching for her baby's pacifier in the middle of the night, then God will abundantly give discernment, understanding, wisdom, and knowledge. Then God's boundaries will become our boundaries.

Honoring Spiritual Boundaries

Spiritual boundaries? What does that mean? Don't we want ourselves and our daughters to grow as deep and wide spiritually as possible? Of course we do. Yet we know that religion can be abused and used to manipulate others. Moms, the best defense we have for protecting our daughters from cults and false religions is the Word of God. We protect them when we teach them the truth, because setting spiritual boundaries requires knowing the truth.

When the FBI trains its officers to identify counterfeit bills, they are taught to recognize every mark and millimeter of the genuine article. By knowing what the real thing looks like, the counterfeit is more easily recognized. When God's Word is read, memorized, and applied to life, then the fraudulent teachings and advice that come our daughters' way will be viewed through a lens of truth and recognized as false. They will be able to make wise choices and know they have freedom to experience all of the incredible things God desires for them in life, within the boundary of His love and commandments.

Colossians 2:8–10 says, "See to it that no one takes you captive through philosophy and empty deception, according to the tradition of men, according to the elementary principles of the world, rather than according to Christ. For in Him all the fullness of Deity dwells in bodily form, and in Him you have been made complete, and He is the head over all rule and authority."

It is only from our own knowledge of God's Word that we are able to teach our daughters. It is only from our own experience with God's presence that we are able to introduce Him to them. And it is only from our own prayer life that we are able to draw the faith, the love, and the hope necessary to provide them with a godly role model, a faithful parent, a lifelong friend.

One morning I woke up early, which was very unusual for me at age fourteen. I went barging into Mom's room to tell her about some new idea I'd dreamed up. All at once I realized that I had interrupted her prayer time—she was on her knees beside her bed. I was a little embarrassed, and I left the room in a hurry. But later we talked about it.

Mom told me that she started every morning in that posture of prayer. Not only is she a gifted attorney and a very active mom, but most of all for many years she has walked closely with the Lord and allowed Him to direct her every step. She is truly a woman who communicates with God.

Through her prayers and her motto for her girls, "You can do *all* things through Christ who strengthens you" (Phil. 4:13, paraphrase), she provided me with the confidence and peace that have stabilized my life. They are not things that I have manufactured; they are truly gifts from God offered to me through my mom's words, prayers, and example.

I am grateful to my mom for living out a life that has modeled "God Power" instead of "Girl Power" as the key to instilling self-confidence, self-control, and strength. She remains a matchless role model for me, and I hope some of the wisdom I originally learned from her will also enrich your life. Let's hope that you and I will be as successful as Mom was in planting within our daughters, from the earliest days of their lives, seeds of faith that will one day blossom into the spirits, souls, and bodies of women of God.

Moms & Daughters: Working It Out Together

1. Discuss physical, emotional, and spiritual boundaries with your daughter, and write them down together. Spend a lot of time listening and gently guiding.

2. Ask if there are times that she has felt she's "crossed a healthy line" in body, soul, or spirit. Share a time when you have found yourself in a compromising place because a boundary was broken. How did you handle it? (Remember not to share details of sexual promiscuity.)

3. Ask if she has ever been spiritually deceived into believing something about God that is not true. Pray together that God will strengthen and protect her faith.

Conclusion

Connecting the Circle,
Creating the Dream

In his book *The Circle Maker,* Mark Batterson, pastor of a large church in the Washington, DC, area, wrote, "Nothing honors God more than a big dream that is way beyond our ability to accomplish. Why? Because there is no way we can take credit for it. And nothing is better for our spiritual development than a big dream because it keeps us on our knees in raw dependence on God."[1]

When a brand-new little baby is placed in our arms for the first time, it's the beginning of a big dream. All we imagine and hope for, which may or may not come true, is wrapped in deep love and a strong desire for God's very best for this precious new life.

God's hand is there in the pain and the uncertainty of birth and parenthood. It is there we find the great joy of a baby and the thrill of growth and adventure. We start to learn to trust in a whole new way—and then they become teenagers!

A decade ago, my oldest was just turning thirteen. It's really wonderful to have the chance to share my experiences again now that the teenage years are almost behind us. Not everything happened as I hoped it would. Some things happened that are so incredible I am still in awe. Some things have happened that I never would have desired for my family, especially my children, to experience.

Knowing the truth and writing it in a published manuscript doesn't mean that real life will follow suit. I know this firsthand! Never would I have imagined that divorce was in my future. Never would I have dreamed that each of my three boys would spend some time in a juvenile detention center or in jail. (Now, by God's grace, each is seeking God with an inspirational fervor.) Never did I imagine that my precious virgin daughter, who loved life, lived it to the fullest, and had a great group of friends, would be abused after school one Thursday afternoon, her life forever altered. Now equipped with great depth and insight, she has walked through the open door to an awesome ministry and outreach to others with similar challenges.

My youngest daughter is a living example that when we learn from each other's mistakes, accept that perfection is not reality, and open our hearts to God so that He can build His truth and principles in us, then our choices will be more aligned with wisdom in a real, down-to-earth way! My "baby girl" is more grounded at sixteen and seventeen than I ever was at that age. She is such a genuine, beautiful young woman!

Sometimes as a mom I feel it's only my kids that go through tough and crazy stuff. It's been such a gift for moms farther down the road to share their stories with me, so I pray this snapshot into our extremely imperfect lives has magnified that you're not alone, giving you an extra dose of encouragement and hope.

When I was a kid, I dreamed of having a "normal" life like my friends. So all I wanted for my kids was to give them a "normal" life, an experience that was stable without too many highs and lows. As you have read, that is not how our lives are playing out. The longer I live, the more I'm not too sure if "normal" really exists. Often families appear to be normal, but that exterior only hides or suppresses the reality of an unfulfilled life. As I talk with friends who have solid, healthy marriages, they say their lives are far from normal. Many say they still pinch themselves because it's hard to believe they get to live the lives they live every day—but those lives are not without some tough times and incredible challenges along with unexpected trials and triumphs.

This year, the devotional *My Utmost for His Highest,* by Oswald Chambers, has had a powerful impact in my life. The November 2 entry, "Obedience or Independence?" is really poignant. The Bible verse, John 14:15, says: "If you love Me, you will keep My commandments." Chambers's entry explains: "The Lord does not give me rules but He makes His standard very clear. If my relationship to Him is that of love, I will do what He says without hesitation. If I hesitate, it is because I love someone I have placed in competition with Him, namely, myself. . . . If I obey Jesus Christ, the redemption of God will flow through me to the lives of others, because behind the deed of obedience is the reality of Almighty God."[2]

How do we live in this fallen world as moms, often feeling as though we're moving from one "crisis" to another? Romans 14 says: "Welcome a man [or woman] whose faith is weak, but not with the idea of arguing over his scruples. . . . Let us therefore stop turning critical eyes on one another. . . . let us be critical of our own conduct and see that we do nothing to make a brother [or sister] stumble or fall" (vv. 1–2, 13 PHILLIPS).

Once again it is clear that the answer is found in honoring the Lord and others by daily seeking obedience through consistent prayer, continually being filled with the Holy Spirit, who lives through our lives.

Living the Different Dream

Will we ever be perfect? Will our daughters?? No! Perfection is not the ultimate goal. What *is* the goal for a Christian woman? Let's be Philippians 1:6 women: "For I am confident of this very thing, that He who began a good work in you will perfect it until the day of Christ Jesus." We will not "arrive" until we reach heaven. Here and now, we are people in process, moment by moment before the Lord, relying on Him for His wisdom, grace, and strength for the next step of the dream of His calling on our lives.

God's dream is a different dream. It doesn't look like the

desires of this world, nor does it look the same for everyone on the surface. At its core, God's vision is the same for everyone who is found by Him and keeps seeking Him as a hidden treasure: it's the vision of letting go of our specific needs and desires, entrusting them all to Him and surrendering to Him completely; hearing His voice; and following and serving Him while watching Him build His dream in us and our daughters, one moment at a time.

Notes

Introduction: Defining the Dream

1. Mary Pipher, *Reviving Ophelia* (New York: Ballantine, 1994).

Chapter 1: Who Am I?

1. *Anastasia*, directed by Don Bluth and Gary Goldman (Los Angeles: 20th Century Fox, 1997).
2. *Titanic*, directed by James Cameron (Los Angeles: Paramount Pictures, 1997).
3. Don and Angie Carter, "False Intimacy vs. True Intimacy," Internet of the Mind, http://www.internet-of-the-mind.com /false-intimacy.html.

Chapter 2: Why Am I Here?

1. *Simon Birch*, directed by Mark Steven Johnson (Burbank, CA: Hollywood Pictures, 1998).
2. George Barna, *The Barna Report: What Americans Believe: An Annual Survey of Values and Religious Views in the United States* (Ventura, CA: Regal Books, 1991), 92, 37.
3. From the author's notes taken during Paige Benton's women's Bible study, Spring 2000.

Chapter 3: What Do I Believe?

1. David E. Kelly, "Faith, Hope & Surgery," *Chicago Hope*, season 6, episode 11, directed by Adam Arkin, aired January 13, 2000, 20th Century Fox Television.
2. David Colbert, ed., *Eyewitness to America* (New York: Vintage, 1998), 642.
3. Mary Pipher, *Reviving Ophelia* (New York: Ballantine, 1994; repr. Riverhead, 2005), 12.
4. Quoted in Iain Murray, *The Forgotten Spurgeon* (Edinburgh: Banner of Truth Trust, 1973), 138.

Chapter 4: What Is Faith?

1. Josh McDowell, *Evidence That Demands a Verdict* (Nashville: Thomas Nelson, 1993).
2. Ibid., 17.
3. Josephus, *Antiquities of the Jews*, 18.3.3, in *The Works of Flavius Josephus*, trans. William Whiston, vol. 3 (Philadelphia: William D. Woodward, 1825), 62.

Chapter 5: Who Is Influencing Me?

1. "Evangelism Is Most Effective Among Kids," Barna Group, October 11, 2004, http://www.barna.org/barna-update /article/5-barna-update/196-evangelism-is-most-effective -among-kids.
2. Sharon Begley, "Why the Young Kill," *Newsweek*, May 3, 1999, 34.
3. Ibid., 35.
4. Ibid.

Chapter 7: Family and Friends

1. *Courageous*, directed by Alex Kendrick (Culver City, CA: TriStar Pictures, 2011).
2. Meri Wallace, *Birth Order Blues: How Parents Can Help Their Children Meet the Challenges of Birth Order* (New York: Henry Holt, 1999), 7–8.

3. Ibid., 8–9.
4. *Wide Awake*, directed by M. Night Shyamalan (New York: Miramax Films, 1998).

Chapter 8: Music and Media

1. Carmen Renee Thompson, "Poll: Teens Rate the Media," *Seventeen*, March 1999, 112.
2. Marisa Grimes, "Nielson: Global Consumers' Trust in 'Earned' Advertising Grows in Importance," Nielson.com, April 10, 2012, http://www.nielsen.com/us/en/insights/press -room/2012/nielsen-global-consumers-trust-in-earned -advertising-grows.html.
3. Neil Postman, *Technopoly* (New York: Vintage, 1993), 18.
4. Andrea Norcia, "The Impact of Video Games on Children," Palo Alto Medical Foundation, http://www.pamf.org /preteen/parents/videogames.html.
5. "Texting While Driving Now Surpasses Drinking and Driving for Teenage Accidents and Fatalities," PRWEB, May 23, 2012, http://www.prweb.com/releases/2012/5/prweb 9530209.htm.
6. Virginia Tech Transportation Institute, "Driver Distraction in Commercial Vehicle Operations," September 2009, http:// www.distraction.gov/research/PDF-Files/Driver-Distraction -Commercial-Vehicle-Operations.pdf, 143.

Chapter 9: Boys and Falling in Love

1. William Shakespeare, *A Midsummer Night's Dream*, 1.1.134. References are to act, scene, and line.
2. Joe S. McIlhaney Jr. and Freda McKissic Bush, *Hooked: New Science on How Casual Sex Is Affecting Our Children* (Chicago: Northfield, 2008), 106.
3. Ibid., 35–36.
4. Ibid., 41.
5. Ibid., 33.
6. Ibid., 43.

Chapter 10: Competition and Complications with Friends

1. Lucy Maud Montgomery, *The Annotated Anne of Green Gables*, ed. Wendy E. Barry, Margaret Anne Doody, and Mary E. Dootdy (New York: Oxford University Press, 1997), 105–6.
2. Dee Brestin, *The Friendships of Women*, 3rd ed. (Colorado Springs: David C. Cook, 2008), 137.
3. Gail McDonald, quoted in Brestin, *The Friendships of Women*, 137.

Chapter 11: School Influence and Grades

1. Mary Pipher, *Reviving Ophelia* (New York: Ballantine, 1994; repr. Riverhead, 2005), 64.
2. Sean Covey, *The 7 Habits of Highly Effective Teens* (New York: Simon & Schuster, 1998), 124.
3. Matea Gold, "A Boot Camp for Troubled Youths," *Los Angeles Times*, June 7, 1999, http://articles.latimes.com/1999/jun/07/local/me-45000.
4. Quoted in Covey, *7 Habits*, 125.
5. Adele Faber and Elaine Mazlish, *How to Talk So Kids Will Listen and Listen So Kids Will Talk* (New York: Avon Books, 1999; repr. Scribner, 2012), 171–73.

Chapter 13: Diet and Exercise

1. Linda M. LeMura and Serge P. von Duvillard, *Clinical Exercise Physiology* (Philadelphia: Lippincott Williams & Wilkins, 2004), 561.
2. Allison Adato, "The Secret Lives of Teens," *Life*, March 1999, 40–41.
3. Selene Yeager and Bridget Doherty, *The Prevention Get Fit, Get Young Plan* (n.p.: Rodale, 2001), 350.
4. Anne Morrow Lindbergh, *The Steep Ascent* (n.p.: Harcourt, Brace, 1944), 22.
5. Marie Anne du Deffand to Jean Le Rond d'Alembert, July 7, 1763, in Gaston Maugras *Trois mois à la cour de Frédéric* (1886).

6. Kristen Stewart, "Does Muscle Weigh More Than Fat?" Everyday Health, May 26, 2010, http://www.everydayhealth .com/weight/busting-the-muscle-weighs-more-than-fat-myth .aspx.

Chapter 14: Weight and Eating Disorders

1. "Eating Disorders: Signs, Symptoms, and How to Help," South Carolina Department of Mental Health, 2006, http:// www.state.sc.us/dmh/anorexia/.
2. "Eating Disorders Among Children," National Institute of Mental Health, http://www.nimh.nih.gov/statistics/1eat_child.shtml.
3. Kim Camp, *Fit to Be Mom* (Nashville: Broadman & Holman, 1996), 57.

Chapter 15: Drugs and Alcohol

1. "Alcohol and Crime," National Council on Alcoholism and Drug Dependence, http://www.ncadd.org/index.php/learn -about-alcohol/alcohol-and-crime.
2. "Drug and Crime Facts," Bureau of Justice Statistics, http:// bjs.ojp.usdoj.gov/content/dcf/duc.cfm.
3. Stephen Arterburn and Jim Burns, *How to Talk to Your Kids About Drugs* (Eugene, OR: Harvest House, 2007), 32.
4. "Blood Alcohol Concentration," In the Know Zone, http:// www.intheknowzone.com/substance-abuse-topics/binge -drinking/blood-alcohol-concentration.html.
5. Linda Foster, "Teen Alcoholism and Drug Addiction," Everyday Health, April 20, 2009, http://www.everydayhealth .com/addiction/addiction-in-adolescence.aspx.

Chapter 16: Sex and Purity

1. Sophie Barton-Knott, "Nearly 50% of people who are eligible for antiretroviral therapy now have access to lifesaving treatment," UNAIDS, November 21, 2011, http://www .unaids.org/en/resources/presscentre/pressreleaseandstate mentarchive/2011/november/20111121wad2011report/.

2. "Aids will kill 68m by 2020, UN says," *Telegraph* (UK), August 29, 2002, http://www.telegraph.co.uk/news /1405708/Aids-will-kill-68m-by-2020-says-UN.html.
3. Associated Press, "How well do condoms work against STDs?" NBCNews.com, June 29, 2005, http://www .nbcnews.com/id/8399212/ns/health-sexual_health/t/how -well-do-condoms-work-against-stds/#.UT3w1M0xZ2k.
4. William Slonecker, personal conversation with the author.

Chapter 17: Style and Body Language
1. Lois Hoadley Dick, *Amy Carmichael: Let the Little Children Come* (Chicago: Moody, 1984), 24, 57.

Chapter 18: Boundaries
1. Beth M. Crissman, *Longing to Belong: Learning to Relate as the Body of Christ*, 2nd ed. (Graham, NC: Plowpoint Press, 2008), 39.
2. "Domestic Violence Statistics," Domestic Violence Resource Center, http://www.dvrc-or.org/domestic/violence/resources /C61/.
3. "Sexual Assault Victimization" (brochure), National Center for the Victims of Crime, https://www.ncjrs.gov/ovc_archives /reports/help_series/pdftxt/sexualassaultvictimization.pdf.

Conclusion: Connecting the Circle, Creating the Dream
1. Mark Batterson, *The Circle Maker* (Grand Rapids: Zondervan, 2011), 43.
2. Oswald Chambers, *My Utmost for His Highest: Updated Edition* (Grand Rapids: Discovery House, 1992), November 2.